THE EVERYDAY
SQUASH COOK

THE EVERYDAY SQUASH COOK

THE MOST VERSATILE & AFFORDABLE SUPERFOOD

ROB FIRING, IVY KNIGHT & KERRY KNIGHT

WITH PHOTOGRAPHY BY REENA NEWMAN

Collins

Published by Collins, an imprint of HarperCollins Publishers Ltd

First edition

All photographs © 2014 Reena Newman with the exception of the following:
pages vi–vii, 14–18 and 39, © 2014 Christopher Campbell; and pages ii, v, viii, x, xii–1, 2, 4, 10–11, 12, 28–29,
80–81, 120–21, 169, 195, 196–97, 198, 200–201, 202, © 2014 Pat Crocker.
Food styling by Chantal Payette.

HarperCollins books may be purchased for educational, business,
or sales promotional use through our Special Markets Department.

HarperCollins Publishers Ltd
2 Bloor Street East, 20th Floor
Toronto, Ontario, Canada, M4W 1A8

www.harpercollins.ca

Library and Archives Canada Cataloguing in Publication
information is available upon request

ISBN 978-1-44342-446-2

Printed and bound in China
PP 9 8 7 6 5 4 3 2 1

For Sherry
—RF

For Rose Marie and Marthe
—IK

For Joan
—KK

CONTENTS

FOREWORD

At first glance, you might think squash is just a vegetable and this is just a book, but look closer and you'll discover one of the world's tastiest and most versatile vegetables and a trove of easy-to-use recipes.

As a Canadian, I treasure the many moments each and every day when we come together and share flavours. Food is one of the most important parts of our cultural identity, and squash has been a welcome guest at the table for thousands of years.

As a cook I strive to create tasty, nutritious food, so I always appreciate when my ingredients are easy to find and easy to prepare. On Prince Edward Island during squash season, all you have to do is leave your car unlocked on the street and when you return it'll be stuffed with fresh local squash and a recipe will be tucked onto your windshield!

As a father I embrace the opportunity to do my best in the kitchen, to pass on knowledge, wisdom and health. None of which works when you cook something your kids won't eat. That's why I love squash—because they do!

Turn the pages, find a recipe you'd like to try and prepare to impress yourself in your own kitchen as you join the authors in elevating the humble squash to its true rock-star status!

Chef Michael Smith
Prince Edward Island

INTRODUCTION

NATURE'S UNSUNG MIRACLE

To many of us, the mention of squash translates first to the indoor racquet sport, and second to a mushy side dish served as an afterthought at holiday dinners once or twice a year. This is a shame because squashes are certainly one of the tastiest and most cookable, handsome, affordable and nutritious foods one can find, and they are readily available in their many wonderful varieties in grocery stores nearly all year long.

Squashes are categorized by growing season into either winter or summer varieties. Summer squashes ripen more quickly and are generally harvested when the fruit is less mature. Winter squashes—those generally larger, thick-skinned varieties—are harvested in the late summer and fall. Their hard outer flesh means they ship very well and can be stored for extended periods of time without refrigeration while keeping their good looks, flavour and nutritional qualities.

In *The Everyday Squash Cook* we focus on nine of the most common varieties of squash. Most of our recipes call for winter squash, but summer squashes, especially zucchini, make appearances throughout. We even have a recipe for their flowers—a special seasonal treat.

In addition to being delicious, squash is one of the most nutritious cultivated foods on the planet. By volume, its level of vitamin A surpasses that of almost all other foods. Squash is also high in vitamin B6, potassium, manganese and many other essential vitamins and minerals. The good news doesn't stop there: the fruit is also loaded with health-protective properties, including those derived from cucurbitacins, powerful anti-inflammatory, antifungal and antioxidant compounds unique to the squash family, used in medicine to help treat and prevent cancers. Pound for pound, you can't name another food that is as nutritious and easily available as the noble squash.

We came together to write this book because we each embrace squash in different ways using our different skill sets: Kerry's mother, Joan, is a wonderful baker, and she raised her son right—that's why most of the recipes for breads, muffins and sweets originated from him. Rob is the gardener, so he provided the research on the many different varieties of squash and their nutritional properties. Rob is also a griller, and those recipes where a barbecue or grill come into play are all his. Ivy is the chef, and she drew on her ten years of experience in professional kitchens to compile the master list of recipes and to test each one with Kerry in their home kitchen. The recipes were tested again by Chantal, the food stylist who worked on the photo shoot for the book. All of the recipes were a hit with the photo crew, and we're sure they'll be a hit with you and your crew at home.

The Everyday Squash Cook aims to equip you with all of the information you need to prepare sumptuous dishes and entire meals for your family and friends. Kid-friendly snacks, appetizers, soups, quick breads, salads, entrées, classic mainstays and some fun and unexpected tricks of the trade are all included. Every recipe in this book is designed to work for busy home cooks, even those who have never prepared this superfood before. So what are you waiting for? Grab a squash and join us in the kitchen.

A NUTRITIONAL POWERHOUSE

With almost five times the recommended daily dose of vitamin A—and a host of other vitamins, minerals, micronutrients and antioxidants—squash gets high marks as one of nature's superfoods. Winter squashes, such as pumpkin and butternut squash, are especially good for us. Just a single serving (about 7 ounces) of butternut squash has more than 450% of the daily recommended value of vitamin A, which we need to maintain good vision and eye health, strengthen our immune systems, maintain healthy skin and mucous membrane cells and even fight cancer (vitamin A inhibits the development of DNA in cancer cells).

Different kinds of squash have different nutritional properties, some of which are completely unique to squash. Where butternut and other orange squashes are higher in vitamin A, others are higher in vitamin C, potassium, vitamin B6, manganese, thiamin and magnesium (see "Meet the Squashes," page 13, for more details).

Most squashes have a healthy balance of carbohydrates and fibre and very little fat content (except for the seeds, which contain healthy oils). For example, 1 cup of roasted or canned pumpkin contains 19.8 grams of carbohydrates and 7.1 grams of dietary fibre. The Heart and Stroke Foundation recommends we consume between 21 and 38 grams of fibre each day. Fibre is good for our digestive system and helps regulate cholesterol and blood sugar levels. Since fibre stays in our digestive system longer than other foods we eat, it slows down the rate at which we absorb sugars from carbohydrates. That means high-fibre foods like squash can effectively lower carbohydrate count.

The glycemic index (GI) measures the rate at which a given food is converted into blood glucose. The higher the GI, the more quickly the food is converted to sugar, which causes a spike in blood sugar levels. This spike triggers insulin release, which can lead to weight gain and fatigue. Glycemic load (GL), however, is a more useful number, as it also measures the actual amount of carbohydrate in food. For instance, watermelon has a high GI because the carbohydrate in watermelon is quickly converted to blood sugar, but it also has a low GL because there isn't that much carbohydrate in it. A cup of spaghetti squash has a low GL of 2, whereas a cup of cooked spaghetti has a GL of 23. Choosing spaghetti squash over pasta is not only a tasty and healthy option, it's better for managing your blood sugar and helping prevent weight gain.

Most squashes also contain cucurbitacins, natural health-protective compounds unique to the squash family that can taste quite bitter in high concentrations. Squashes have evolved to produce cucurbitacins in their tissues in order to be less palatable to herbivores. Some wild varieties of squash have high levels of the compound, and anyone who has tried tasting a gourd—definitely not recommended—will know how bitter the experience can be. If you want a better way to experience the taste of this remarkable compound, try biting into a piece of raw butternut squash, in the thinner "neck" section. Uncooked, the sugars in the squash are unconcentrated, and the dry, bitter taste of the cucurbitacins comes through.

At very high levels, cucurbitacins are toxic to mammals, but squashes have been cultivated to produce it in much lower levels. (An exception is the squash relative bitter melon, a kind of cucumber popular in some Chinese cooking, whose bitter taste is part of the vegetable's overall appeal.) It is difficult to determine the exact levels of cucurbitacins in any respective squash since concentrations can vary depending on the conditions where the squash was grown.

Recent research has found that curcubitacins have powerful beneficial effects, including cancer-fighting, anti-inflammatory and hepaprotective (liver-protective) properties. The majority of the research available today tends to focus on cancer prevention and cancer treatment. Curcubitacins inhibit the growth of cancer cells on different fronts, making the compound potentially useful in combination with other cancer therapies. Cucurbitacins are heat resistant and not readily water soluble, so their health properties remain just as potent when the squash is cooked.

All of this is good news for us, since curcubitacin levels are just high enough in squash for us to enjoy the beneficial properties, but low enough for us to enjoy squash's rich, sweet flavour. It's just one more reason why squash is not to be overlooked when it comes to nutritional value.

VITAMINS AND MINERALS FOUND IN SQUASH

Vitamin A: fights cancer, combats acne, maintains vision, boosts immune system

Vitamin B6: fights heart disease, lessens the effects of PMS, maintains brain and nerve health, essential for healing

Vitamin B1 (Thiamin): fights heart disease, lessens the effects of PMS, maintains brain and nerve health, essential for healing

Vitamin C: antioxidant, fights cancer, boosts immune system, boosts fertility in men

Magnesium: helps us absorb calcium, boosts energy, detoxifies

Manganese: helps with the formation and health of bones and connective tissue, essential in processing carbohydrates, cholesterol and protein

Potassium: regulates blood pressure, needed for muscle strength and kidney function

Tryptophan: fights depression, helps regulate sleep, not often found in plants

Phosphorus: necessary for healthy kidney function and bone health

Copper: necessary in the formation of red blood cells and the function of many internal organs

Zinc: maintains healthy hormone levels, regulates sugar and salt cravings, necessary in cell division, slows aging

Iron: necessary for protein metabolism, red blood cell and hemoglobin formation, and healthy immune system

Eat the Skin!

The skin of most winter squash is very edible

when cooked and loaded with dietary fibre.

Try roasting peelings with the seeds

for a crispy, nutritious snack.

MEET THE SQUASHES

Each variety of squash has special characteristics that make it unique. Some become fibrous when lightly cooked and can be peeled away from their skin in spaghetti-like strands; others are dense with a drier, darker flesh. Some are long-necked and therefore easier to peel and cut; others are moist and slightly spongy, which is great for puddings and pies. Some have plump seeds with thinner shells and are ideal for roasting; others are tender and ready to eat raw in the summer.

One thing that can be said for sure is that squashes are incredibly versatile. They're also quite forgiving. Their nutty flavours work well with warm spices like nutmeg, clove and even curry. Their earthy flavours love aromatic herbs and tangy cheeses. If you're not already a squash cook, you may be pleasantly surprised by the breadth of dishes to which they are suited. You haven't lived until you've had squash for breakfast!

Whenever possible, we offer substitutions for any of the varieties we use in the recipes. There are certainly many great types of squash available for sale, especially at farmers' markets. We encourage you to try them all, keeping in mind that, generally speaking, the darker the flesh, the denser and sweeter the fruit. The following are the nine varieties we have found to be most commonly available in North American supermarkets.

ACORN

Cucurbita pepo

Sometimes called pepper squash, acorn squash gets its name from its shape: flat on top, wide around the middle then narrowing to a tapered end, like an acorn. Its tough, smooth skin is ridged and dark green, often with an orange patch along its side (although you can also find some new coloured varieties). The flesh is light amber and sweet-flavoured. When halved and roasted (the skin is edible), acorn squash is very tasty and perfect for stuffing. Its seeds are good for roasting.

Recommended daily values of vitamins and minerals in 1 cup cooked acorn squash: 18% vitamin A; 23% vitamin B1 (thiamin); 20% vitamin B6; 37% vitamin C; 9% calcium; 11% iron; 22% magnesium; 22% manganese; 24% potassium.

BUTTERNUT

Cucurbita moschata

One of the most popular squashes in North America, butternut squash ripens to a bright orange. Faint green stripes on the flesh indicate the squash was picked before it was ripe, so look for uniform orangey-beige skin. The long neck of this squash is seedless, making it easy to cut and peel. The raw juice is bitter and feels slightly astringent on the tongue, but this disappears when it's cooked. The skin is sometimes tougher on large examples, but generally edible when roasted with the flesh. The flesh is sweet but not quite as dense as some other varieties. Like most winter squash, its seeds are delicious roasted.

Recommended daily values of vitamins and minerals in 1 cup cooked butternut squash: 457% vitamin A; 52% vitamin C; 8% calcium; 7% iron; 18% magnesium; 18% manganese; 17% potassium. Also a good source of vitamin B1 (thiamin), vitamin B6, vitamin E, folate and niacin.

CHAYOTE

Sechium edule

Especially popular in the Caribbean and Central and South America, chayote squash is roughly the size of a pear, pale green and shaped like a slightly flattened ball with one puckered lip. Sometimes called a christophine, it is generally considered a summer squash despite being almost always eaten cooked and harvested when fully mature. Some varieties are sandy in colour with a column of spiky protrusions along their sides. The flesh is almost white and stays crisp at first when cooked through, similar to a water chestnut.

Recommended daily values of vitamins and minerals in 1 cup cooked chayote squash: 21% vitamin C; 14% manganese. Also a good source of folate, pantothenic acid (also known as vitamin B5, another essential vitamin) and potassium.

HUBBARD

Cucurbita maxima

The *Cucurbita maxima* species is, as the name suggests, the largest winter squash. Some are large enough to be entered in contests at country fairs. The 'Golden Hubbard' (pictured here) is one of our favourites and is generally available at markets, farm stands and better supermarkets in the fall and winter. Hubbards are among the densest varieties of squash, making them among the tastiest and most nutritious as well. The largest kinds are often sold in pre-cut wedges. There are many subvarieties in this family of squash, within which nutritional values can vary. While some are orange, hubbards are often dark green to pale greyish blue, with tapered ends. The seeds are great roasted.

Recommended daily values of vitamins and minerals in 1 cup cooked hubbard squash: 247% vitamin A; 18% vitamin B6; 32% vitamin C; 3% calcium; 5% iron; 18% manganese; 20% potassium. Also a good source of magnesium.

KABOCHA
Cucurbita maxima

Popular in Japan, kabocha is a very close relation to hubbard and buttercup squash (different cultivars of the same species). It originated in Indonesia and was likely brought there by the Portuguese via the Americas. The skin is quite tough, often with rough knobbly bits. Its flesh is deep orange, dense and has a taste that is more distinctive than most other squashes. Its dark-coloured flesh means that it's loaded with vitamin B. It is sweet tasting and holds up well during cooking, so it can easily sub in for potato or sweet potato in soups and stews.

Recommended daily values of vitamins and minerals in 1 cup cooked kabocha squash: 247% vitamin A; 18% vitamin B6; 32% vitamin C; 3% calcium; 5% iron; 18% manganese; 20% potassium. Also a good source of magnesium.

PATTYPAN
Cucurbita pepo

Pattypan squashes, sometimes picked very young (baby squash), have a scalloped edge resembling a crown and are shaped almost like a spinning top. Baby squashes are about the size of a peach pit and are easily steamed, boiled or sautéed. Larger pattypans are grapefruit size and can be sliced and fried or grilled like zucchini. The seeds are not yet developed in these immature summer squashes.

Recommended daily values of vitamins and minerals in ½ cup cooked pattypan squash, including skin: 20% vitamin A; 7% vitamin C; 1% calcium; 2% iron. Also a good source of vitamin B1 (thiamin), vitamin K, copper, folate, magnesium, manganese, phosphorus and potassium.

PUMPKIN

Cucurbita pepo, Cucurbita mixta, Cucurbita maxima and *Cucurbita moschata*

Cultivated in the United States, pumpkins are a derivation of other varieties of winter squash, notably hubbard and kabocha. Pumpkins range considerably in size, from a pound or less up to 450 pounds, the biggest appearing as amusing news items nearly every fall. Their thick skin is most often orange, but there are white, grey and red varieties. The flesh is pale orange, firm and slightly spongy with a higher moisture content than most other squash. They absorb flavour well and are wonderful in both sweet and savoury recipes. Their plentiful seeds are perfect for roasting; the relatively thin shells contain lots of "meat." Pumpkins must be planted in warm temperatures and so are the last squashes to be harvested—just in time for Halloween and Thanksgiving.

Recommended daily values of vitamins and minerals in 1 cup canned pumpkin: 763% vitamin A; 17% vitamin C; 6% calcium; 19% iron; 14% manganese. Also a good source of vitamin E, vitamin K, copper, magnesium, pantothenic acid (also known as vitamin B5, another essential vitamin), phosphorus and potassium.

SPAGHETTI

Cucurbita pepo

So called because its fibrous flesh separates into spaghetti-like "noodles" once cooked, spaghetti squash is a great substitute for pasta and is wonderful roasted, forked into strands and sautéed or served cold in salads. The skin of this football-shaped winter squash ranges in colour from light yellow to light orange.

Recommended daily values of vitamins and minerals in 1 cup cooked spaghetti squash: 3% vitamin A; 9% vitamin C; 3% calcium; 3% iron. Also a good source of vitamin B6, vitamin C, manganese, niacin, pantothenic acid (also known as vitamin B5, another essential vitamin) and potassium.

ZUCCHINI & CROOKNECK

Cucurbita pepo

Both of these summer squashes are tender-fleshed and thin-skinned, perfect for quick cooking but also good served raw in salads or shaved into "pasta" ribbons. They are generally harvested immature—they can get really big, especially zucchini, which can grow to over three feet in length—and are available locally in temperate climates during the summer. Zucchini is usually green, but yellow crookneck varieties show up in supermarkets in the summertime. The zucchini flower is slow to mature. Because of this, and because the plants are prolific and quite easy to grow, the flowers are often harvested and used in salads or battered and fried tempura-style.

Recommended daily values of vitamins and minerals in ½ cup cooked zucchini, including skin: 20% vitamin A; 7% vitamin C; 1% calcium; 2% iron. Also a good source of vitamin B1 (thiamin), vitamin K, copper, folate, magnesium, manganese, phosphorus and potassium.

THE STORY OF SQUASH

Squash is indigenous to the Americas, and the word itself derives from one of the several Algonquian families of languages. *Askútasquash*, in the Narragansett language of what is now Rhode Island, was simply shortened to *squash* by European settlers. Mentions of squash first appeared in European colonial records in the early 1600s.

Archeological records indicate that squash was first cultivated in Central and South America as far back as 8,000 to 10,000 years ago, though there is much earlier evidence of squash as a staple crop for the great Native American civilizations, including the Maya, Inca, Aztec and later, farther north, the Iroquois, Huron and others.

Many Native American societies grew squash in proximity to beans and maize (corn) using a technique known today as companion planting. When the maize was tall enough to provide support, beans and squash were planted alongside. While the bean vines climbed the maize stalks in search of sun, their roots trapped vital nitrogen in the soil through symbiotic bacteria called rhizobia, which accumulated in nodules in the vine's roots. Meanwhile, the slightly sticky and hairy squash vines and leaves deterred insect pests from infesting the companion plants; the large leaves of the squash vines also shaded the soil, keeping it moist.

Squash, beans and corn are often referred to as "the three sisters" because of their symbiotic relationships. We now also know that each crop provides nutritional values that the others lack: Beans provide essential amino acids, such as tryptophan and lysine, not present in corn. Corn provides carbohydrate value. Squash provides abundant levels of vitamin A and other important nutrients. Those interested in following a Paleo diet would do well to incorporate these tried-and-true "sisters" into their meal plans.

TECHNIQUES FOR HANDLING

Anyone who has cut open a watermelon—or carved a jack-o'-lantern for that matter—knows that preparing big fruit can be a bit awkward. Once you get the hang of it, you'll realize how quick and easy it can be and wonder why it took you so long to become a squash cook.

HALVING & SEEDING ACORN SQUASH

1. First, make sure your hands are towel dry, so the squash won't slip. Make sure your cutting surface is stable and dry, too. Hold the squash firmly in place. Using a sharp chef's knife, slice off the stem end as close to the end of the curve as you can, about a ¼ inch. Do the same to the tapered end.

Tip: If your cutting board is wobbly or slides when you use it, place a folded kitchen towel underneath the cutting board to help keep it in place.

2. Turn the squash on its now-flat head and slice ¼ inch from the round side of the acorn squash—just enough to create another flat surface.

Tip: Once you get some practice, you can forgo cutting off the side slice and simply use the flat surface cut from the stem end to stand the squash on its head. Then bring the knife down through the squash, starting from the trimmed tapered end.

3. Turn the squash on its side to rest on the flat surface you've created. Push the knife through, making sure the blade of the knife is facing away from your other hand, as pictured here.

4. Slowly lever the knife down through the squash until the knife is in contact with your cutting surface. Remove the knife and rotate the squash 180 degrees, still on its side-cut surface.

5. Repeat the steps: push the knife through, meeting your first cut, and lever the knife down away from your hand until the squash is cut in half.

6. Using a wooden spoon, scoop out the loose fibre and seeds. You don't have to be too fussy with the loose fibre if there is some left attached.

HALVING & SEEDING BIGGER SQUASH

1. Make sure your hands are dry and your cutting board is steady. Use a sharp chef's knife to slice off the ends and one side of the squash (a spaghetti squash is shown here).

2. Rest the squash flat-side down. Gently but firmly push the blade of the knife into the side of the squash with your palm (be careful to keep your fingers out of the way) until the blade breaches the squash's skin and sinks into the flesh a little.

3. Take a wooden meat pounder or rubber mallet and tap the knife, gently at first, into the flesh of the squash.

4. Keep tapping the knife until it goes all the way through and the squash is cut in half.

5. Next, remove the seeds and all of the loose fibre.

6. For best results, try scraping out the cavity with the snap lid of a Mason jar.

PEELING SQUASH & MAKING SQUASH RIBBONS

Using a Y-shaped speed peeler (preferred) or a regular vegetable peeler, peel strips down the length of the zucchini to create "pasta" ribbons. (Try them in the recipe for Zucchini Salad on page 100.)

Using a Y-shaped speed peeler (preferred) or regular vegetable peeler, peel the skin from the elongated end of the butternut squash and discard. Then, peel ribbons of flesh down its length. (Try them in the recipe for Butternut "Bacon" on page 38.)

SIMPLE SQUASH RECIPES TO GET YOU STARTED

Many recipes in *The Everyday Squash Cook* call for some type of prepared squash as an ingredient. The following truly simple instructions for cooking squash four different ways, plus a recipe for roasting pepitas, will equip you for making the recipes in this book and incorporating squash into your mealtimes more frequently.

ROASTED SPAGHETTI SQUASH

When a recipe calls for "roasted spaghetti squash" (see Spaghetti Pie on page 106) we mean a spaghetti squash that has been cooked through well enough for spaghetti-like strands to form easily, but not so much that the "noodles" break down. Here's how to do it.

Halve and seed the squash as demonstrated in "Halving & Seeding Bigger Squash" (page 22). Spread a teaspoon of olive oil or other vegetable oil on the exposed cut surface of the squash, using the spoon or your fingers so that the cut surface is evenly coated. Don't worry if you get some oil in the cavity. Place both halves of the squash cut-side down on a baking sheet lined in parchment paper. Bake in a preheated 400°F oven for 20 minutes. Remove from the oven. Using the tines of a dinner fork, claw the flesh of a halved and roasted spaghetti squash lengthwise into "noodles." If the spaghetti strands do not form easily, continue cooking for another 5 minutes at a time until they do. Be careful not to overcook spaghetti squash or you'll lose that great stringy texture.

Spaghetti squash does not freeze well, but you can cook it in advance and store it in the refrigerator for 2 to 3 days.

ROASTED CUBED SQUASH

Some recipes call for "roasted cubed squash." By that we mean a squash that has been peeled, cut into cubes and roasted. (This is also a tasty and nutritious side dish on its own. Try it with salt, pepper and olive oil and, if desired, a spice of your choosing.)

Cut, seed and peel the squash as demonstrated in "Techniques for Handling" (pages 20–23). Carefully cut the squash crosswise (across its width) into ¾-inch slices, and then cut those slices into cubes. Your cubes don't have to be perfectly geometrical, but try to keep them roughly the same size to ensure even cooking.

Lightly coat the squash with olive oil or other cooking oil and season with a big pinch of salt. Spread the squash evenly on a baking sheet lined in parchment paper. Roast in a preheated 400°F oven for 10 to 15 minutes, then turn the cubes over and roast for an additional 10–15 minutes or until tender. Turning is recommended to ensure even browning.

You can cube most varieties of winter squash when it's raw and store in a resealable bag in the freezer for roasting later. Just be sure to add an extra 5 to 10 minutes to the cooking time, if cooking from frozen.

Tip: We use roasted cubed squash in most of our recipes because it retains more flavour, but cubed squash can also be boiled. Cut, seed and peel the squash, and then cut into cubes as described above. Bring a saucepan filled with enough water to cover squash, plus 1 teaspoon kosher salt, to a rolling boil. Add squash, and cook for 6 to 10 minutes, or until tender. Drain well. Use the boiled squash as you would roasted squash. For savoury recipes, add an onion, halved, and a bay leaf to the water along with the squash. Reserve the cooking water to use as vegetable stock.

ROASTED SQUASH FOR STUFFING

Roasted acorn squash is so versatile, and there are countless ways to stuff it (see our recipe for Acorn Stuffed Five Ways, page 148). Use the following method to roast all types of winter squash for stuffing.

Halve and seed the squash (see "Techniques for Handling," pages 20–23). Place it cut-side down on a parchment-lined baking sheet. Roast in a preheated 350°F oven until just tender, about 40 minutes, or until the flesh is fork tender. Remove from the oven and spoon your desired stuffing into the squash. Return to oven for 6 to 8 minutes to cook the stuffing. Either enjoy immediately or store in an airtight container and refrigerate for 2 to 3 days, until needed (just warm it up in the oven before serving).

MASHED OR PURÉED ROASTED SQUASH

Mashed or puréed roasted squash is great on its own and as a thickener for soups, stews and sauces. You can freeze it in ice-cube trays, then empty the trays into resealable bags and return to the freezer for later use.

Cut and seed any variety of squash—butternut, acorn, hubbard or kabocha work best—as demonstrated in "Techniques for Handling" (pages 20–23). Spread a teaspoon of olive oil or other vegetable oil on the exposed cut surface of the squash, using the spoon or your fingers so that the cut surface is evenly coated (don't worry if you get some oil in the cavity). Place both halves of the squash cut-side down on a baking sheet lined in parchment paper. Bake in a preheated 400°F oven until tender, about 30 minutes. Test by inserting a fork into the flesh. If the fork does not sink easily through, right to the skin, cook for another 10 minutes or until it does.

Remove from the oven and set aside to cool enough so that you can safely scoop out the flesh from the skin. Mash by hand using a potato masher until reasonably smooth, or purée in a food processor fitted with a metal blade. Add ¼ cup of water at a time to achieve your desired consistency.

PAN-ROASTED PEPITAS

Pepitas are the seeds of squash or pumpkin with the shells removed. They are great raw (and more nutritious that way) but are also really fantastic roasted. Some of our recipes call for "roasted pepitas" (they also make a delicious, nutritious, kid-friendly snack by themselves—just add a little salt, if you like).

In a dry medium frying pan, cook 1 cup or more of raw pepitas (the seeds should be no more than two layers thick) over medium-high heat, stirring them around occasionally to ensure even cooking, for about 3 minutes. You will know they are done when they lose their olive-green colour, becoming a little darker and browner, and start to lightly pop in the pan, becoming slightly rounder and hollow inside. This happens quite quickly so be sure to watch carefully. Remove from the heat and immediately transfer the seeds to a bowl to cool completely. Store in an airtight container at room temperature.

STORING SQUASH

Because of their thick skin and sturdy structure, whole winter squashes can be stored at room temperature for up to 3 months, sometimes even longer. In fact, refrigerating whole winter squashes can reduce their shelf life considerably, as moisture can condense on their surface and cause early rotting. Keep them dry and out of direct sunlight.

While freezing spaghetti squash does not work particularly well (it loses its wonderful stringy texture), other winter squashes do hold up well to freezing after they've been peeled and cut into pieces. You can save a lot of time by having cubed squash on hand in a resealable bag in the freezer. Drop the cubes into soups and stews, or use frozen cubed squash in any of the recipes in this book that call for it, making sure to add 5 to 10 minutes cooking time as needed.

Summer squashes such as pattypans and crooknecks don't freeze well and are best eaten fresh (raw or cooked). Refrigerate summer squashes if you are keeping them for longer than a day. Store them whole in the fridge. Don't be afraid of canned or frozen pumpkin (or any canned or frozen squash, for that matter); it is conveniently precut and cooked, and works wonderfully in many recipes. Interestingly, many canned brands sold as "pumpkin" are not really pumpkin at all, but a deeper-orange variety of related squash called 'Boston Marrow'. This, of course, is just fine. Boston Marrow, part of the hubbard group of squash cultivars, is very tasty and is responsible for the remarkably high levels of vitamin A content in commercial canned pumpkin.

Super Seeds

Pumpkin and squash seeds are high in
zinc, which boosts your immune system, and
in magnesium, which helps your heart, strength-
ens bones and can help control blood sugar levels.
Many North Americans aren't getting enough of
these essential minerals—sprinkle pumpkin
seeds on a salad, or roast them for a
crunchy, nutritious snack.

BREAKFAST & BRUNCH

Whether it's a quick breakfast before you run out the door or a leisurely brunch with family and friends, what you can achieve with squash will astound you. Acorn and eggs, pumpkin and banana, butternut "bacon"—weekend mornings will never be the same again.

Clockwise from top left: Green Smoothie (page 34); Zucchini & Spaghetti Squash Latkes (page 49); Israeli-Style Baked Eggs with Chickpeas & Squash (page 55); Butternut "Bacon" (page 38); Breakfast Strata with Acorn Squash, Cheddar & Ham (page 56); and Breakfast Tacos (page 47).

GREEN SMOOTHIE

This lovely pale green smoothie is a frothy, creamy dream, so it's shocking to discover that it's completely dairy-free. (Photo on pages 30–32.)

MAKES 2 SERVINGS

1 green apple (Granny Smith), cored and chopped

1 cup pure apple juice

½ cup grated or chopped zucchini

½ cup seedless green grapes

½ cup crumbled medium-firm tofu

1 tablespoon flaxseed, pumpkin seed, avocado or almond oil

Liquid honey, to taste

Put all of the ingredients in a blender and blend on high speed until smooth. If the smoothie seems too thick, add more juice.

Tip: Always keep flaxseed oil refrigerated so that it doesn't go rancid.

CANTALOUPE BUTTERNUT ALMOND SMOOTHIE

Kerry loves to whip up this smoothie before rowing or playing tennis. It's very filling and perfect for those crazy mornings when you don't have time to eat. A touch of maple syrup will make it a favourite breakfast treat. We suggest you double this recipe (see Tip).

MAKES 2 SERVINGS

1 cup chopped cantaloupe

1 cup roasted cubed butternut squash (see page 25)

¼ cup plain yogurt

1 cup orange juice

1 tablespoon almond butter, peanut butter or Wow butter

1 tablespoon pure maple syrup or liquid honey

Put all of the ingredients in a blender and blend on high speed until smooth.

Tip: Store extra smoothie in a jar in the fridge and shake vigorously before serving. No need to haul out the blender.

BANANA BUTTERNUT BLUEBERRY SMOOTHIE

The tofu in this smoothie provides lots of protein, which translates into lots of energy to start your day. It's truly a meal in a glass.

MAKES 2 SERVINGS

1 banana
½ cup roasted cubed butternut squash
   (see page 25)
½ cup crumbled medium-firm tofu
½ cup fresh blueberries

1 tablespoon flaxseed, pumpkin seed,
   avocado or almond oil
Liquid honey, to taste (optional; see Tip)
1 cup orange juice

Put all of the ingredients in a blender and blend on high speed until smooth. If the smoothie seems too thick, add more juice.

Tip: When blueberries are in season and sweet, you may choose to omit the honey. At other times, like during the dead of winter, you may want to add a dash of sweetness. You can also substitute an equal amount of Concord grapes for the blueberries.

APPLE PUMPKIN MUFFINS

These robust muffins combine the classic autumnal flavours of pumpkin and apple cider, and are the perfect thing to make on a cool fall morning. They're also quick and delicious—a no-brainer.

MAKES 12 MUFFINS

1¾ cups all-purpose flour

1 teaspoon baking soda

¼ teaspoon baking powder

1 teaspoon ground cinnamon

¼ teaspoon ground nutmeg

½ teaspoon kosher salt

¼ cup butter, softened

1 cup granulated sugar

2 eggs

½ cup applesauce

½ cup canned unsweetened pumpkin purée

⅓ cup apple cider

½ teaspoon pure vanilla extract

½ cup raisins

Preheat the oven to 375°F. Line a 12-cup muffin pan with paper liners.

In a medium bowl, mix the flour, baking soda, baking powder, cinnamon, nutmeg and salt.

In another bowl, beat the butter and sugar until creamy, then mix in the eggs, applesauce, pumpkin, cider and vanilla. Gently stir in the dry ingredients—do not over-mix. Fold in the raisins.

Spoon the batter into the prepared muffin cups until three-quarters full. Bake in preheated oven for 20 to 25 minutes or until a toothpick inserted into the middle of a muffin comes out clean. Remove from the oven and let cool in pan for 5 minutes, then turn out onto a wire rack to cool completely.

Tip: The secret to great muffins is not over-mixing the batter. You want to stir in the ingredients just until combined—no more—so they bake up rather rustic with large air pockets for melting butter.

BREAKFAST MUFFINS WITH ZUCCHINI, BACON & CHEDDAR

Kerry makes these muffins in double batches and freezes half. They are so addictive, it's good to have lots on hand. They are packed with the goodness of zucchini, yogurt, sharp cheddar cheese and the irresistible allure of smoky bacon—a meal you can hold in one hand!　　MAKES 12 MUFFINS

3 cups all-purpose flour

1 tablespoon granulated sugar

4 teaspoons baking powder

1 teaspoon fresh cracked black pepper

1 teaspoon kosher salt

1 cup milk

½ cup plain yogurt

⅓ cup olive oil

2 eggs

1 cup grated zucchini

¼ cup chopped green onion, white and green parts

1 cup shredded sharp (old) cheddar cheese

5 strips crispy bacon, crumbled

Preheat the oven to 375°F. Line a 12-cup muffin pan with paper liners. Set aside 1 tablespoon cheese and 1 tablespoon bacon for topping the muffins.

In a medium bowl, mix the flour, sugar, baking powder, pepper and salt.

In another bowl, mix the milk, yogurt, oil and eggs until well combined. Mix in the zucchini, green onion, cheese and bacon. Gently stir in the dry ingredients—do not over-mix.

Spoon the batter into the prepared muffin cups until three-quarters full. Sprinkle with the reserved bacon and cheese. Bake in preheated oven for 25 to 30 minutes or until a toothpick inserted into the middle of a muffin comes out clean. Remove from the oven and let cool in pan for 5 minutes, then turn out onto a wire rack. Serve warm.

BUTTERNUT "BACON"

When Rob told us about butternut "bacon," we were skeptical—nothing can compare to the king of breakfast meats! But Rob showed us that butternut "bacon" can come pretty close. This is an amazing vegan recipe for the easiest and most magical-tasting fake bacon ever. Set it out on a platter and watch it disappear . . .   **MAKES 24 TO 36 "BACON" STRIPS**

1 butternut squash, peeled and seeded
Grapeseed, peanut or vegetable oil

Kosher salt and fresh cracked black pepper

Using a Y-shaped vegetable peeler, peel the butternut squash. Next, peel the flesh into long strips, applying firm pressure for adequate thickness. Peel as many strips as you wish (about 6 to 8 strips per person); reserve any unused squash for another dish.

In a frying pan, heat 1/8 inch of oil (just enough to "float" the squash strips) over medium heat. Once the oil is shimmering, carefully place the a few strips of squash in the pan, being careful not to over-crowd. (We recommend doing a trial strip first, as butternut "bacon" cooks extremely quickly.)

Cook the bacon, flipping once, until the edges are lightly browned and a little crispy, about 10 to 15 seconds per side. Be careful not to overcook—dark, fully crisp "bacon" will taste burnt.

Transfer the cooked "bacon" to a plate lined with paper towel to absorb excess oil. (If cooking a large batch, keep warm in a low oven.) Season to taste with salt and pepper.

Tip: Try putting 2 or 3 strips of butternut "bacon" on top of a serving of green salad—it's a simple, elegant and tasty garnish. We also like to use any extra we have on hand in Breakfast Tacos (page 47) and BLTs (page 88).

SPEEDY PUMPKIN WAFFLES

Adding puréed pumpkin to that buttermilk pancake mix you have in the pantry not only tastes great, but also adds vitamins A, C and K, as well as iron, potassium and dietary fibre. It's like having pumpkin pie for breakfast! (This mixture works great for pancakes, too.) You can change things up by adding ¼ cup chopped apple, peaches, walnuts or pecans, or blueberries or cranberries.

MAKES 12 FOUR-INCH WAFFLES

1 cup buttermilk pancake mix
1 cup milk
⅓ cup canned unsweetened pumpkin
  purée

1 egg
1 tablespoon melted butter

Place all of the ingredients in a bowl and stir well.
Follow the instructions for your waffle maker, pouring batter in batches onto preheated, oiled waffle iron. Cook until golden, about 3 to 5 minutes. Keep cooked waffles warm in the oven.
Serve warm with butter and maple syrup.

SPEEDY PUMPKIN PANCAKES

Place all of the ingredients in a bowl and stir well. Place an oiled frying pan over medium heat. When the oil is hot, drop about ¼ cup batter per pancake into the pan. Cook until bubbles start to appear on top of the pancakes and the edges begin to brown, 1 to 2 minutes. Flip the pancakes over and cook for 1 to 2 minutes more, until browned on the bottom. Repeat with the remaining batter, adding more oil to the pan as needed. Keep cooked pancakes warm in the oven. Serve warm with butter and maple syrup.

OPEN-FACED PUMPKIN BANANA SANDWICHES

Make these robust open-faced sandwiches on hearty multigrain bread. They're a healthy alternative to chocolate-hazelnut spread in the mornings and have a sweetness kids like. This recipe will yield two sandwiches, but feel free to really load up on the ingredients if you so desire.

MAKES 2 SANDWICHES

4 slices multigrain bread, toasted
2 tablespoons cream cheese
2 tablespoons canned unsweetened
   pumpkin purée

1 ripe banana, sliced
1 tablespoon liquid honey
Ground cinnamon

Spread cream cheese over one side of each piece of toast, then spread a layer of pumpkin purée overtop. Top that with a layer of banana. Drizzle with honey and sprinkle with cinnamon, to taste.

BREAKFAST BISCUITS

For many people, the smell of biscuits baking is more intoxicating than the aroma of bacon sizzling or coffee brewing. Although making biscuits from scratch as soon as you wake up may not be in the cards, you can prepare them the night before and refrigerate them (unbaked) overnight. Then when you roll out of bed all you have to do is pop them in the oven. Doing this on Sunday night so you can have fresh biscuits on Monday morning makes for an amazing start to the week. These aren't your run-of-the-mill biscuits—the squash ensures a lovely, soft crumb.　　　MAKES 20 TO 24 BISCUITS

2 cups all-purpose flour

4 teaspoons baking powder

2 teaspoons granulated sugar

½ teaspoon kosher salt

3 tablespoons shortening, chilled

½ cup grated zucchini

1 teaspoon finely chopped fresh thyme

⅔ cup milk

Preheat the oven to 450°F. Line a baking sheet with parchment paper.

In a mixing bowl, sift together the flour, baking powder, sugar and salt. Using two knives or a pastry blender, cut in the shortening until the mixture resembles cornmeal. Mix in the zucchini and thyme. Add the milk and mix gently with a fork until just combined.

Turn the mixture out onto a floured work surface and gently knead just to bring the dough together. Using a rolling pin, roll out the dough to an even ½-inch thickness. Using a 3-inch biscuit cutter, juice glass or Mason jar lid, cut out rounds. Transfer the biscuits to the prepared baking sheet. (If making ahead, stop here, cover and refrigerate overnight.) Refrigerate for 15 minutes before baking.

Bake in preheated oven for 10 to 12 minutes, rotating the pan at the 5-minute mark to ensure even browning. Bake until golden.

Serve warm with butter (these go great with Mussel Chowder with Summer Squash, page 74) or use to make breakfast sandwiches (recipe follows).

BREAKFAST BISCUIT SANDWICHES (shown right)

These savoury biscuits are delicious on their own, but Kerry likes to use them for making breakfast sandwiches. Warm the biscuits in the oven, split them open and fill with scrambled eggs or Tofu Scramble with Spicy Zucchini (page 50). Add Butternut "Bacon" (page 38), tomato slices, shredded cheese and your favourite fresh greens.

SAVOURY ZUCCHINI POPOVERS

Popovers seem to only ever make an appearance with roast beef dinners, but they're so good and quick to make that we think they deserve to shine at breakfast, too. We should all try to start the day with the smell of freshly baked popovers as often as possible—especially considering how easy they are to whip up in a blender.

MAKES 12 LARGE POPOVERS

1 cup grated zucchini

1½ cups all-purpose flour

1½ cups milk

1 teaspoon kosher salt

3 eggs

3 tablespoons melted butter

Preheat the oven to 450°F. Get out a 12-cup muffin pan and put a teaspoon of some kind of fat in the bottom of each cup (it can be bacon fat or chicken drippings or lard or butter).

Place the zucchini in a colander, sprinkle with salt and toss to mix (the salt will draw the liquid out of the zucchini so it won't make the popover soggy). Let sit for 10 minutes, then, using your hands, wring out the zucchini, squeezing out as much water as possible.

In a blender on high speed, blend the flour, milk, salt, eggs and butter, stopping to scrape down the sides of the blender as necessary, until smooth. Add the zucchini and pulse to combine.

Place the prepared muffin pan in preheated oven and heat until the fat in the bottom of the cups melts and starts to sizzle, about 30 seconds. Carefully remove the pan from the oven and scoop the batter into the muffin cups, filling to the brim. Bake for 14 minutes, then reduce the oven temperature to 350°F and bake for another 15 minutes. Popovers are ready when they are golden brown. Remove from the oven and serve immediately.

BREAKFAST POPOVER SANDWICHES

Just like Breakfast Biscuits (page 44), these popovers make perfect breakfast sandwiches! Simply warm the popovers in the oven, then fill with scrambled eggs or Tofu Scramble with Spicy Zucchini (page 50), Butternut "Bacon" (page 38), tomato slices, shredded cheese and your favourite fresh greens.

BREAKFAST TACOS

Tacos for breakfast? Why not! This is a great way to stretch a batch of Butternut "Bacon" (page 38). The garnishes listed below are suggestions only. Feel free to prepare more or less, depending on how "fat" you like your tacos, and to substitute your favourite ingredients—building them is half the fun! (Photo on pages 30–32.)

MAKES 8 TACOS

Garnishes
16 strips Butternut "Bacon" (page 38)
½ cup shredded cheddar cheese
1 tomato, chopped
1 red bell pepper, seeded and sliced
½ avocado, pitted and sliced
¼ red onion, diced
¼ cup mixed fresh cilantro and parsley
   leaves

Sour cream
Salsa
Hot sauce

8 small corn or flour tortillas
Knob of butter
4 eggs (see Tip)

Prepare your garnishes and place them in serving bowls.

Preheat the oven to the lowest setting. Wrap tortillas loosely in foil and place in oven to warm, 2 to 3 minutes.

In a frying pan over medium heat, melt the butter and scramble the eggs to desired doneness.

Serve up everything on the table and build your tacos.

Tip: One egg scrambled should be enough for 2 tacos once you add all of the other garnishes.

GRILLED CHEESE SANDWICHES WITH PUMPKIN & BRIE

Want a grilled cheese tip from a pro? Ivy never ever uses anything other than salted butter to cook her grilled cheese sandwiches. In this take on a classic, we pair up soft and creamy brie with nutty Parmesan—the two work wonderfully with the earthy flavour of pumpkin and the tart, crisp apple. Tailor the ingredient amount to suit your tastes, and serve sandwiches with some Butternut Chutney (page 151) for dipping.

Puréed roasted pumpkin (see page 26) or canned unsweetened pumpkin purée
Bread (2 slices per sandwich)
Apple, cored and cut into thin slices

Parmesan cheese
Brie (2 slices per sandwich)
Butter (preferably salted)

Spread the pumpkin purée over one slice of bread and top with apple slices. Grate Parmesan over the apple and top with sliced brie. Butter another slice of bread and place, buttered-side up, on top of the sandwich.

Heat a frying pan over medium-high heat, melt some butter in the pan and place the sandwiches, buttered-side up, in the pan (the bottom will cook in the melted butter). Cook until the bottom is golden brown, 2 to 3 minutes. Flip and let that side brown up as well. Once they're toasted and melty, transfer them to a cutting board, slice and serve.

ZUCCHINI & SPAGHETTI SQUASH LATKES

You can whip up these delicious latkes in just a few minutes provided you've got some roasted spaghetti squash ready to go. Serve with fruit salad, applesauce and sour cream or rich Greek yogurt. (Photo on pages 30–32.)

MAKES 6 LATKES

1½ cups lightly packed grated zucchini

1 cup packed roasted spaghetti squash, forked into "noodles" (see page 24)

1 green onion, white and green parts, chopped

1 teaspoon kosher salt

Fresh cracked black pepper

1 egg

1 tablespoon all-purpose flour

1½ tablespoons olive oil

While heating a frying pan over medium-high heat, combine all of the ingredients—except the oil—in a bowl and mix well.

Once the pan is hot, pour in the oil and swirl to coat the pan. Scoop the latke mixture into the pan (a soup-spoonful is a good amount; you should be able to fit 4 latkes into the pan at one time) and cook until golden brown on both sides, about 1 minute per side.

Transfer the latkes to a serving plate. (If you're doubling the batch, you can place the latkes on a wire rack set over a cookie sheet and keep warm in a low oven.) Repeat with the remaining latke mixture. Serve warm.

TOFU SCRAMBLE WITH SPICY ZUCCHINI

The secret to this vegan alternative to scrambled eggs might surprise you. Marmite, a food spread made from yeast extract, is an optional ingredient, but don't dismiss it until you try it—what a difference it makes when it meets tofu! (Vegemite works too.) Marmite is high in B vitamins and packs an unmistakable hit of umami, just the trick for amping up the somewhat timid flavours of zucchini and tofu. We didn't include a quantity for the Marmite because it's too sticky to measure conventionally. Just stick a clean fork into the jar and coat the tines about halfway, then press the fork into the scramble and let the heat melt the Marmite as you stir. This recipe works really well as a filling for breakfast burritos.

MAKES 2 SERVINGS

1 tablespoon olive oil
1 cup zucchini, cubed
Kosher salt and fresh cracked black
  pepper
6 to 8 cherry tomatoes, halved
2 tablespoons chopped roasted red bell
  pepper (store-bought is fine)

½ teaspoon hot pepper flakes (or to
  taste)
1 cup crumbled medium-firm tofu
Marmite optional (see headnote)

Heat the oil in a frying pan over medium-high heat (see Tip). Drop in the zucchini. Season with salt and pepper to taste. Sauté the zucchini until browned, about 4 minutes. Transfer the cooked zucchini to a plate.

To the hot pan, add the tomatoes, red pepper and hot pepper flakes and sauté for 1 minute. Add the tofu and stir to combine. Stir in the Marmite (if using) and the cooked zucchini. Serve immediately.

Tip: The key to cooking delicious zucchini is a hot pan so the cubes brown quickly before they overcook. Think of it like searing meat for a stew.

TOAST BASKETS FILLED WITH CHEESY SCRAMBLED EGGS & BUTTERNUT "BACON"

Ivy first discovered the recipe for toast baskets filled with scrambled eggs in her mother's home-ec book from the 1960s. The Teen Guide to Homemaking *had a number of gelatin salad recipes that caught her eye, but this breakfast recipe has become a staple in the Knight house. To make toast baskets you need really soft supermarket bread.*

MAKES 4 BASKETS

4 slices fresh bread
12 to 16 pieces Butternut "Bacon" (see page 38; use 3 to 4 per basket)
2 eggs

2 tablespoons milk
Knob of butter
½ cup tomato, chopped
½ cup shredded cheddar cheese plus extra for topping

Preheat the oven to 350°F. Get out a 6-cup muffin pan.

Trim the crusts from the bread (save crusts for another use). Using a rolling pin, roll the bread to half its original thickness (this makes it easy to shape). Spread each rolled slice with butter. Using your fingers, gather the four corners of the bread together (to make a "basket") and then place each basket in a muffin cup butter-side in, spreading out the four corners to drape over the pan. Bake in preheated oven for 5 to 8 minutes, until golden brown.

Meanwhile, cook the "bacon."

In a small bowl, whisk together the eggs (1 egg will be enough to fill 2 baskets) and milk. Heat a frying pan over medium heat and melt the butter. Add eggs and cook until scrambled, stirring in tomato and cheese at the end.

Remove the pan from the oven and divide the egg mixture among the baskets. Top with additional cheese and finish with "bacon." Return to the oven and bake for 2 to 3 minutes, until the cheese is melted. Serve immediately.

POACHED EGGS OVER SQUASH & GREEN TOMATO MASALA HASH

This is an excellent dish to make if you have a good supply of unripened (green) tomatoes in your garden. Even though they aren't as sweet tasting as ripe tomatoes, green tomatoes can be used to great effect in cooking. They have a unique, slightly tart, vegetal taste. Use them to make fried green tomatoes or this exotic breakfast hash that incorporates the flavours of tandoori masala.

MAKES 2 SERVINGS

1 dash of white vinegar
Olive oil
1 medium green tomato, chopped
1 cup roasted cubed butternut squash
　　(see page 25)

1 green onion, white and green parts,
　　chopped
1 tablespoon tandoori masala (spice mix)
4 eggs
Naan bread
Kosher salt

Prepare to poach your eggs: Bring a saucepan of salted water to a boil over medium heat and add the vinegar (the vinegar will help to set the egg whites).

While you are waiting for the water to boil, heat a little oil in a frying pan over medium heat. Add the tomato, squash and the white part of the chopped green onion and stir gently to combine. Stir in the tandoori masala and cook for 3 to 5 minutes. Set aside and keep warm.

Crack the eggs into a small bowl (this makes it easier to quickly pour them into the poaching water). Once the water in the saucepan is at a steady, relaxed boil it is time to add the eggs.

Before you plop the eggs into the saucepan, give the water a circular stir to get it moving in one direction (this helps the eggs to coalesce as they hit the water, keeping their whites closer to their yolks). Then pour the eggs slowly into the water, dropping them in one by one. Depending on how you like your eggs, leave them to cook (without stirring) for 2 to 4 minutes (about 2 minutes for soft-poached eggs, 4 minutes for firm eggs).

While the eggs are poaching, pop some naan into a low oven or toaster oven to warm and brown.

Scoop the masala hash into shallow serving bowls and tuck some toasted naan on the side. Using a slotted spoon, carefully lift the poached eggs from the water and arrange two eggs over each serving. Sprinkle with the green onion and a pinch of salt. Serve immediately.

ISRAELI-STYLE BAKED EGGS WITH CHICKPEAS & SQUASH

Shakshuka is a traditional Israeli breakfast dish made by poaching eggs in a sauce of tomato, onion and garlic. We like to add squash and chickpeas for extra flavour, texture and nutrition. (Photo on pages 30–32.)   **MAKES 2 SERVINGS**

1 tablespoon olive oil

½ small onion, finely chopped

1 clove garlic, minced

1 cup tomato sauce (store-bought is fine)

½ cup roasted cubed butternut squash (see page 25)

½ cup canned chickpeas, rinsed and drained

Kosher salt and fresh cracked black pepper

4 eggs

2 pita bread

Chopped fresh parsley leaves, for garnish

Hot sauce

In a cast-iron frying pan with a lid, heat the oil over medium-high heat. Add the onion and garlic and sauté until fragrant, about 1½ minutes. Add the tomato sauce, squash and chickpeas. Season with salt and pepper to taste. Cook, stirring often, until heated through, about 5 minutes. Make 4 nests in the sauce using a wooden spoon and crack the eggs into the nests. Reduce the heat to medium and cover pan with the lid. After 3 to 4 minutes lift the lid to check the eggs (the egg whites should be fully set).

Meanwhile, warm pita in a low oven or toaster oven just before serving.

Scoop the eggs out with the tomato stew and divide between two plates.

Sprinkle with parsley and hot sauce. Serve with the warmed pita bread.

BREAKFAST STRATA
WITH ACORN SQUASH,
CHEDDAR & HAM

This breakfast casserole is one of Rob's favourites and a great dish to make over the holidays, ideal for mornings when company is in the house. It can be assembled the night before, so all you have to do is wake up, whip it into the oven, make some coffee and get some juice. By the time the table is set, the strata should be ready to serve. Since it includes all the breakfast standards— eggs, bread, some form of pork—you don't need to worry about serving anything else. It's a great way to use up any stale bread you have, and sneaking the squash in gives the strata a nice texture, added nutrition and an extra hit of flavour.   MAKES 6 SERVINGS

1 loaf bread
1 cup chopped cooked ham
1 cup mashed roasted acorn squash
  (see page 26)
2½ cups shredded sharp (old) cheddar
  cheese, divided

6 eggs
2 cups milk
½ teaspoon kosher salt
½ teaspoon fresh cracked black pepper

Grease a 9- × 13-inch casserole dish or large deep-dish pie plate.

Tear the bread into bite-size pieces and place in a bowl. Add the ham, squash and 2 cups cheese and stir well. Spoon the mixture into the prepared baking dish.

In the same bowl, whisk together the eggs, milk and salt and pepper. Pour over the bread mixture and stir just to combine. Cover the strata with foil or plastic wrap and refrigerate overnight, stirring once before bed.

In the morning, remove the strata from the fridge, give the mixture a stir and preheat the oven to 375°F.

Sprinkle the strata with the remaining ½ cup cheese and bake in preheated oven for 45 minutes or until puffed and golden. Serve warm.

DIPS & SOUPS

Squash was made for soup, in all seasons. It whips up into a delightful purée, whether it's zucchini and watercress served cold on a hot sunny day or butternut stewed with apple cider and cheddar for a cold winter's night. We add squash to chili, chowder and stew—and just wait till you try it in dips! We bet you never thought of adding squash to guacamole or whizzing it up with smoked trout and cream cheese. Try any of these recipes once and you'll be a convert.

Clockwise from top left: One-Avocado Guacamole for a Crowd (page 64); Hearty Beef, Barley & Butternut Squash Stew in a Bread Bowl (page 73); Super-Fast Butternut Soup & 20 Garnishes (page 72); Roasted Red Pepper & Squash Dip (page 62); and Smoked Trout Dip (page 63).

ROASTED RED PEPPER & SQUASH DIP

This dip contains only six ingredients, but they come together to create a deliciously complex and addictive flavour. Using jarred roasted red pepper saves on prep time, or you can toss a fresh pepper in the oven while the squash cooks. (Photo on pages 58–60.) **MAKES ABOUT 2 CUPS**

⅓ cup chopped roasted red bell pepper (store-bought is fine)

½ cup puréed roasted acorn squash (see page 26) or canned unsweetened pumpkin purée

½ cup cream cheese (see Tip)

Fresh lemon juice

Kosher salt and fresh cracked black pepper

In a food processor fitted with the metal blade, combine the roasted red pepper, squash and cream cheese and blitz until smooth. Add lemon juice and season with salt and pepper to taste. Pulse to combine. Scrape into a serving bowl. Serve with veggies and crackers.

Tip: One ½-pound brick of cream cheese is enough to make two dips, so use half for this dip and the other half for Smoked Trout Dip (page 63). Bonus: If you make the dips in that order, you won't need to clean the food processor in between (no trout will get into the vegetarian dip, and the trout dip will benefit from a bit of roasted pepper in the mix).

SMOKED TROUT DIP

This dip tastes great made with either acorn or kabocha squash. We find the milder taste of acorn works best, but the sweetness of kabocha isn't bad either! Experiment and see what you like. (Photo on pages 58–60.)

MAKES ABOUT 2 CUPS

½ cup smoked trout (see Tip)
1 cup puréed roasted acorn or kabocha squash (see page 26)
½ cup cream cheese (see Tip, page 62)
1 green onion, white and green parts, chopped

Kosher salt and fresh cracked black pepper
Fresh lemon juice
¼ cup chopped fresh parsley leaves or dill fronds (optional)

In a food processor fitted with the metal blade, combine the smoked trout, squash, cream cheese and green onion and blitz until smooth. Taste and adjust the seasonings with salt and pepper (see Tip). Add lemon juice to taste and herbs (if using) and pulse to combine. Scrape into a serving bowl. Serve with veggies and crackers.

Tip: You can use any smoked fish you like, just be careful with your seasoning: some smoked fish may be salty enough from the smoking process.

ONE-AVOCADO GUACAMOLE FOR A CROWD

Only one ripe avocado in the house and a crowd of people looking for something to dip their tortilla chips into? Not to worry! With this recipe you can stretch that one avocado to make a new version of guacamole that will please everyone. (Photo on pages 58–60.) MAKES ABOUT 2 CUPS

1 ripe avocado, pitted and mashed
1 chayote squash, peeled and finely diced
1 green onion, white and green parts, minced
Fresh juice of ½ lime

Kosher salt and fresh cracked black pepper
1 bunch of fresh cilantro leaves, chopped (optional)

In a bowl, combine the avocado and chayote. Stir in the green onion and lime juice. Season with salt and pepper to taste and stir in cilantro (if using). Serve with tortilla chips.

CHILLED CUCUMBER & ZUCCHINI SOUP

No cooking required! Just chop, blend, refrigerate and serve. This soup is a must-have for dinner on the patio on a hot summer night. Serve it with grilled kebabs and a big salad for dinner al fresco with lots of chilled white wine.

MAKES 6 SERVINGS

2 cups chopped zucchini

2 cups chopped seedless cucumber

2 green onions, white and green parts, chopped

¼ cup water

¼ cup white wine vinegar

½ cup crème fraîche or plain Greek yogurt (see Tip)

Chopped fresh mint, for garnish

Combine the zucchini, cucumber and green onions in a bowl. Combine the water and vinegar in a measuring cup. Working in two or three batches, purée the vegetables in a blender, adding the water and vinegar mixture as needed to reach desired consistency. Season to taste and stir in the crème fraîche. Cover and refrigerate to cool before serving. Pour into serving bowls and garnish with fresh mint.

Tip: Crème fraîche is easy to make at home. Add 1 tablespoon fresh lemon juice to 1 small carton (8 oz) whipping (35%) cream. Simply open the cap on the carton, pour in the lemon juice, seal tightly, shake well and let sit at room temperature overnight. When you check it in the morning you'll see how thick it is. Refrigerate until it's time to use (créme fraîche will keep in the refrigerator for 2 weeks).

QUICK ZUCCHINI & WATERCRESS SOUP

This soup comes together almost too fast! Have the blender at the ready and ask everyone to sit down at the table. By the time the onion has softened in the pan, you're almost done making the soup. The bright, fresh green colour is stunning, and it's achieved by just barely cooking the green ingredients in this recipe.

MAKES 6 SERVINGS

1 tablespoon olive oil

1 onion, finely chopped

1 clove garlic, minced

3 cups chicken or vegetable stock

2 to 3 zucchini, roughly chopped

1 cup frozen green peas

1 bunch of fresh watercress, chopped (stems and all)

1 tablespoon (18%) cream plus more for garnish

Kosher salt and fresh cracked black pepper

Chopped fresh mint, for garnish

In a large saucepan, heat the oil over medium-high heat. Add the onion and garlic and cook, stirring occasionally, until the onion is softened, about 1½ minutes. Add the stock and bring to a simmer. Add the zucchini and peas, stir to combine, and bring the soup back to a simmer. Stir in the watercress and turn off the heat.

Using a slotted spoon, transfer the onion, zucchini, peas and watercress to a blender, reserving the cooking liquid in the pan. To the blender, add the cream and ½ cup cooking liquid. Purée on high speed until smooth. Return the puréed mixture to the saucepan, stir well and season with salt and pepper to taste.

Ladle into serving bowls and garnish with a splash of cream and a sprinkling of mint.

Tip: Be sure to rinse the watercress well. No need to trim the stems, as they'll purée nicely in the blender.

BUTTERNUT, WHITE BEAN & ESCAROLE SOUP

This soup is hearty and filling, comes together in a flash and tastes like something you've been slaving over for days. The secret? Source a good beef stock from a local butcher—it will have more beef flavour and, often, less salt (but a box of your favourite ready-made stock will work, too). Escarole resembles a head of leaf lettuce but has tougher leaves; it is hearty and a tiny bit bitter, perfect in this soup.

MAKES 6 TO 8 SERVINGS

1 tablespoon olive oil

1 onion, finely diced

2 ribs celery, including leaves, finely diced

1 clove garlic, minced

8 cups beef stock (see headnote)

2 cups peeled cubed butternut squash

½ cup quinoa, rinsed and drained (see Tip)

2 bay leaves

1 can (19 oz) white beans (cannellini, navy or white kidney beans), rinsed and drained

1 cup chopped zucchini

1 head escarole, chopped

In a frying pan, heat the oil over medium-high heat. Sauté the onion, celery and garlic until fragrant, 2 to 3 minutes. Add the beef stock, squash, quinoa and bay leaves and stir to combine. Bring to a boil, reduce the heat and simmer for 10 minutes. Stir in the beans and cook for 10 minutes, until quinoa is tender.

Add the zucchini and escarole stirring well (the escarole may look like it won't fit in the pot, but it will wilt down quickly). Return to a simmer and cook for 1 minute. Discard the bay leaves. Serve immediately.

Tip: The surface of quinoa contains saponins, which are a bitter compound. To remove, simply rinse (don't soak) the quinoa before cooking.

SPAGHETTI SQUASH SOUP WITH COCONUT MILK & GINGER

This Thai-inspired soup comes together in minutes. You can use homemade stock or store-bought, and canned coconut milk. The addition of soy sauce and rice vinegar at the end gives the soup a more complex flavour. When serving, Ivy likes to set out the lime wedges and chopped chiles, peanuts and cilantro on a lazy Susan in the centre of the table so everyone can use as much or as little of each garnish as they want.

MAKES 4 TO 5 SERVINGS

1 tablespoon olive oil

1 small onion, finely diced

1 teaspoon minced fresh gingerroot

1 clove garlic, minced

4 cups chicken stock

1 can (14 oz) coconut milk

½ large roasted spaghetti squash, forked into "noodles" (see page 24)

1 teaspoon soy sauce

1 teaspoon rice vinegar

Garnishes

Lime wedges

Chopped fresh Thai chiles

Chopped roasted unsalted peanuts or cashews

Chopped fresh cilantro leaves

In a frying pan, heat the oil over medium heat. Sauté the onion, ginger and garlic until fragrant, about 1½ minutes. Pour in the chicken stock and coconut milk and stir to combine. Stir in the spaghetti squash "noodles" and simmer for 10 minutes. Remove the pan from the heat and stir in the soy sauce and vinegar.

Ladle soup into serving bowls. Serve with garnishes alongside.

SQUASH, APPLE & CHEDDAR SOUP

This soup by Rossy Earle, the retail chef kitchen manager at Toronto's Ryerson University and one of the chefs on the kitchen team at CBC's Steven and Chris show, is sure to become a favourite. It incorporates the best flavours of autumn—squash and apples—and crowns them in cheddar, a beautiful combo.

MAKES 6 TO 8 SERVINGS

2 tablespoons olive oil

½ cup garlic cloves

1 large onion, diced

1 large apple, peeled and diced

1 large butternut squash, roasted and mashed (see page 26)

¼ cup pure maple syrup

Pinch of ground nutmeg

½ cup apple cider

4 cups chicken or vegetable stock

1 bay leaf

1 cup whipping (35%) cream

1 cup shredded cheddar cheese plus more for garnish

Kosher salt and fresh cracked black pepper

Crème fraîche, sour cream or plain Greek yogurt (optional)

Chopped fresh chives, for garnish

In a large soup pot, heat the oil over medium heat. Add the garlic, onion and apple and cook, stirring often, until the onion is translucent and apple is soft, 3 to 5 minutes. Stir in the squash, maple syrup and nutmeg. Deglaze with the apple cider (see Tip).

Stir in the stock and bay leaf and bring to a boil. Reduce the heat and simmer for about 10 minutes. Turn off the heat and discard the bay leaf.

Using an immersion blender or food processor fitted with the metal blade, purée until smooth. Return the mixture to the pot. Stir in cream and bring to a boil, then reduce the heat to low. Whisk in the cheese, until melted. Season with salt and pepper to taste. If desired, add a bit more apple cider.

Ladle into serving bowls. Top with a dollop of crème fraîche (if using). Sprinkle with extra cheese and chives. Serve immediately.

Tip: To deglaze a pan, add liquid, usually stock or wine, and stir to dissolve the cooking sediments from the bottom of the pan, capturing robust, concentrated flavours.

SUPER-FAST BUTTERNUT SOUP & 20 GARNISHES

Company's coming and nothing's prepared! While you put the family to work cleaning the house, you have to throw something together quickly to feed a crowd. No problem. Make this simple soup and serve with several of the garnishes listed below. Throw some bread and a salad on the table, and you've got dinner. Your guests will enjoy customizing their soups, and you'll be able to sit down and relax. The possibilities are endless: chorizo and sweet corn, curry powder and lime zest, bacon and blue cheese, yogurt and pomegranate molasses, sour cream and chipotle with corn nuts, freshly grated cheese . . . (Photo on pages 58–60.)　　　　　　　　　　　　　　　　**MAKES 6 SERVINGS**

1 tablespoon olive oil

1 butternut squash, peeled, seeded and chopped

1 onion, chopped

8 cups chicken stock

2 bay leaves

Garnishes

Bacon, crumbled

Blue cheese, crumbled

Chipotle, chopped

Chorizo, chopped

Corn kernels

Corn nuts

Croutons

Curry powder

Fresh chiles, chopped

Fresh herbs (chives, chervil, dill), chopped

Ham, cubed

Hard cheese, grated (Parmesan, Romano, Grana Padano)

Lime zest

Onion or alfalfa sprouts

Pesto

Plain Greek yogurt or sour cream

Pomegranate molasses

Roasted cashews

Salsa

Spiced pumpkin seeds

In a large saucepan over medium-high heat, heat the oil. Sauté the squash and onion until the onion is softened, about 1½ minutes. Add the chicken stock and bay leaves, cover and bring to a boil. Reduce the heat and simmer until the squash is soft, about 10 minutes. Discard the bay leaves.

Purée using a stand or immersion blender. Return the soup to the pan (if needed) and keep warm over low heat.

Arrange a selection of garnishes in bowls on the table. Ladle the soup into serving bowls and enjoy.

HEARTY BEEF, BARLEY & BUTTERNUT SQUASH STEW IN A BREAD BOWL

Serving a stew in one large bread bowl looks great but can be hard to share. We prefer big hearty buns placed in individual bowls. The addition of frozen peas is a secret learned from Kerry's mother, Joan. Adding them at the last minute cools the soup so you don't burn your tongue, and they give the stew a hit of colour. (Photo on pages 58–60.)   MAKES 4 TO 6 SERVINGS

1 pound stewing beef, cut into 1-inch
   cubes
Kosher salt and fresh cracked black
   pepper
2 tablespoons olive oil
1 onion, chopped
2 ribs celery, chopped
1 clove garlic, minced
1 tablespoon all-purpose flour
1 cup red wine

4 cups beef stock
½ cup pearl barley
1 cup peeled and cubed pepper squash
2 bay leaves
1 teaspoon chopped fresh rosemary
   leaves
4 to 6 large fresh buns
Olive oil
½ cup frozen peas

Pat the stewing beef dry using paper towels. Season well with salt and pepper.

In a large heavy-bottomed saucepan or Dutch oven, heat the oil over medium-high heat. Working in two batches so as not to crowd the pan, sear the beef on all sides. Transfer the cooked beef to a plate.

Reduce the heat to medium and, in the same pan, add the onion, celery and garlic (add more oil if needed). Sprinkle with the flour and sauté until fragrant, about 2 minutes. Deglaze with the red wine and cook for 5 minutes (see Tip, page 70). Stir in the beef stock, barley, squash and bay leaves. Bring to a simmer and cook for 15 minutes, until barley is tender. Add the rosemary and reserved beef to the pan and continue to cook for another 15 minutes.

Meanwhile, preheat the oven to 350°F. While the oven is heating, prepare the bread bowls. Slice a circle off the top of each bun and hollow out the centre, being careful not to remove too much (reserve the top crusts and bread pieces for another use). Brush the inside of your bread bowls with oil and place on a baking sheet. Bake in preheated oven for 3 to 5 minutes, until just toasted. Remove from the oven and place each bread bowl in a shallow soup bowl.

Before serving, discard the bay leaves and stir the peas into the simmering stew. Remove the pan from the heat and ladle the stew into the prepared bread bowls. Serve immediately.

MUSSEL CHOWDER WITH SUMMER SQUASH

Ivy grew up on Prince Edward Island, where chowder is traditionally made with clams, potatoes and bacon. That's a great combination, but we felt like a change, so we added summer squash, which grows plentifully there, and replaced the clams with the famed PEI blue mussels. We didn't mess with the potatoes or bacon, though—they're the bits that make chowder so addictive.

MAKES 6 SERVINGS

2 to 3 strips bacon, cut into ½-inch pieces
½ onion, chopped
2 to 3 ribs celery, chopped
8 cups chicken stock
2 bay leaves
1½ cups cubed Yukon Gold potatoes

1 pound mussels, rinsed (see Tip)
1 cup cubed zucchini or pattypan squash
½ cup half-and-half (10%) cream (or whole milk if preferred)
Chopped fresh herbs such as thyme, chives or dill (optional)

In a large saucepan over medium-high heat, cook the bacon until crispy, 5 to 8 minutes. Using a slotted spoon, transfer the bacon to a plate lined with paper towel.

Sauté the onion and celery in the bacon fat until they begin to soften, 2 to 3 minutes. Add the stock, bay leaves and potatoes. Bring to a boil, reduce the heat and simmer for 10 to 15 minutes, until the veggies are tender. Add the mussels and squash, then cover the pan with a lid. The mussels will cook within 2 minutes. Taste, adjust the seasoning with salt and pepper to taste (you probably won't need to add much salt; the mussels and bacon should perfectly season the whole pot). Remove from the heat, discard the bay leaves and any unopened mussels and stir in the cream. Garnish with fresh herbs (if using). Serve immediately.

Tip: Fresh mussels should close when you give them a tap. Discard any that remain open. Scrub them under cold water and trim off any beards before cooking.

MARTHE'S CHICKEN STEW
WITH SQUASH DUMPLINGS

Ivy's Acadian grandmother, Marthe Mailloux, née Bois, is 95. She still lives at home and cooks every day for herself and her friends, Electa, Fernand, Nicole and Thérèse, who come over for nightly card games of Madame du Pic. Marthe simply calls this stew "bouillon" and says that it was a staple in her family. It will continue to thicken the longer it sits, but the dumplings won't disintegrate. This stew is absolutely fantastic the next day.

MAKES 6 SERVINGS

Stew
1 tablespoon olive oil
1 whole chicken, cut into 8 pieces
    (2 thighs, 2 drumsticks and 2 breasts,
    halved)
Kosher salt and fresh cracked black
    pepper
1 onion, diced
2 cloves garlic, thinly sliced
1 cup white wine
3 cups chicken stock

2 bay leaves
2 zucchini, chopped

Dumplings
1 cup mashed roasted acorn, hubbard
    or butternut squash (see page 26) or
    canned unsweetened pumpkin purée
Kosher salt and fresh cracked black
    pepper
1 cup all-purpose flour

In a large heavy-bottomed saucepan, heat the oil. Add the chicken and season with salt and pepper to taste. Sear the chicken on all sides, until browned, then transfer to a plate and set aside.

Add the onion and garlic to the pan and sauté until softened, about 1½ minutes. Deglaze with the white wine (see Tip, page 70). Add the stock and bay leaves. Return the chicken to the pan. Bring the soup to a simmer and cook for 10 to 15 minutes, until the chicken is cooked through. Using a slotted spoon, transfer the chicken to a plate, reserving the stock in the pan (keep it at a simmer). Discard the bay leaves. At this point you can pick the chicken meat off the bones (discarding the skin and bones), or you can leave the chicken pieces as is, depending on how rustic you like your stew.

Make the dumplings: In a bowl, season the squash with salt and pepper to taste. Stir in the flour until well combined.

Drop the dumpling batter (it will be sticky) by the small spoonful into the simmering stock (you should be able to fit about a dozen or so dumplings in the pan). Give the stew a gentle stir and let the dumplings simmer for about 5 minutes. Stir in the zucchini and cook for 1 to 2 minutes, until heated through. Return the chicken to the pan and heat through. Serve immediately, making sure each person gets at least 2 dumplings.

PORK, SQUASH & WHITE BEAN CHILI

Replacing some of the legumes traditionally used in chili with butternut squash (diced to a similar size) adds a subtle sweetness and makes this version more nutritious without increasing calories. Rob likes to serve this with the Cheesy Squashy Cornbread (page 194).   **MAKES 8 TO 12 SERVINGS**

1 pound medium ground pork

1 onion, chopped

1 can (28 oz) diced tomatoes, with juice

1 can (5½ oz) tomato paste

2 cups peeled cubed (½ inch) butternut squash

1 clove garlic, minced

1½ tablespoons chili powder

½ teaspoon cayenne

½ teaspoon ground cumin

2 bay leaves

2 teaspoons salt

1 teaspoon fresh cracked black pepper

1 can (14 oz) cannellini or white kidney beans, rinsed and drained

In a large saucepan over medium-high heat, cook the ground pork until browned, about 8 minutes. Pour off all the fat except about 2 tablespoons. Reduce the heat to medium and stir in the onion. Cook until the onion is browned, about 3 minutes. Add the tomatoes, breaking them up with the back of the spoon. Stir in the tomato paste. Add the squash, garlic, chili powder, cayenne, cumin, bay leaves, salt and pepper and stir to combine. Reduce the heat to low, cover and cook for 15 to 20 minutes, stirring occasionally. Stir in the beans and continue to cook until the squash is tender, about 15 minutes.

Potassium Fix

One medium-sized zucchini has 500 mg
of potassium—as much as an average banana,
and more than a cup of fat-free milk. Potassium
can reduce blood pressure and the risk of stroke
and help your body process excess salt.

MAIN COURSES

Squash is a natural and colourful complement to many dishes, adding a richness sometimes lacking in rice or potato sides, transforming a simple meal into something really special. These recipes showcase how well squash works with savoury flavours, smoky tones and tangy tastes while adding fewer carbohydrates and more nutritional value than the usual suspects.

Top left to right: Zucchini Salad (page 100); Fish Cakes (page 100); Roast Chicken Stuffed with Squash & Wild Rice (page 112) ; and Savoury Buttercup & Sausage Bake with Currants (page 118).

SQUASH BURGERS

A great veggie burger should cover all the bases without making you feel like you're missing out on the "real thing": it should hold its shape, be easy to cook and, above all, taste delicious. These burgers are all of that and more, and can be cooked from frozen in the same amount of time! Don't try to cook these on a grill; they'll fall through. Fry them in a pan. MAKES 6 QUARTER-POUND BURGERS

¼ cup olive oil, divided

½ onion, chopped

1 can (19 oz) black beans, rinsed and drained

¼ teaspoon ground cumin

1 teaspoon kosher salt

1 teaspoon fresh cracked black pepper

½ teaspoon Worcestershire sauce

2 teaspoons soy sauce

1 cup mashed roasted acorn squash (see page 26)

½ cup cooked brown rice

½ cup cooked pearl barley

1 egg (see variation below)

½ cup dried breadcrumbs

In a frying pan, heat 2 tablespoons oil over medium heat. Sauté the onion for 1½ minutes, until softened. Add the beans, cumin, salt, pepper, Worcestershire and soy sauce, stirring with a spatula to break up the beans a little. Remove from the heat and stir in the squash, rice and barley. Add the egg and mix well. Stir in the breadcrumbs.

Divide the mixture into 6 even portions and, using your hands (lightly oil them to prevent sticking), roll each portion into a ball. Using the palm of your hand, flatten each ball to form a patty ½ inch thick.

In an oiled frying pan, cook the burgers for 6 minutes on each side. Serve on hamburger buns with all the fixings.

VEGAN SQUASH BURGERS

For a vegan version, substitute 1½ tablespoons cornstarch combined with 4 tablespoons water (or liquid reserved from the canned beans) for the egg.

Tip: Make a big batch and freeze to keep on hand for whenever the mood for a burger strikes. Stack the patties with parchment or waxed paper between them so they don't stick together when frozen.

BUTTERNUT SQUASH
SANDWICHES TWO WAYS

CHICKEN SALAD SANDWICHES (shown right)

Serve these chicken sandwiches unconventionally: folded up in naan bread like tacos. Of course, you can also use pita or sliced bread, but soft, warmed naan transforms these into something special.

MAKES 4 LARGE SANDWICHES

4 naan bread

2 cups cooked chicken, cooled

¼ cup chopped toasted pecans (see Tip)

½ cup roasted cubed butternut squash
   (see page 25)

1 green onion, white and green parts,
   chopped

Dijon mustard

Mayonnaise

Garnishes

Sunflower or alfalfa sprouts

Onion, diced (optional)

Warm naan in a low oven.

In a large bowl, combine the chicken, pecans, squash and green onion. Stir in Dijon mustard and mayonnaise, to taste.

To serve, scoop a generous amount of the chicken salad onto one half of the naan, top with your choice of garnishes and fold naan over like a taco. *Voila!*

Tip: A great way to bring out the flavour of nuts is to toast them in a dry frying pan over medium-high heat. Toss and cook, keeping an eye on them, until they smell toasty, 2 to 3 minutes. Remove from heat and set aside to cool. Chop and use as needed.

BEST VEGGIE BLT! (shown left)

For the best veggie BLT ever, toast 2 slices of your favourite bread, slather one with mayo, top it with some fresh lettuce and thick slices of ripe tomato, finish with Butternut "Bacon" (see page 38) and crown it with the other piece of bread. Enjoy!

GIANT FOCACCIA SANDWICH WITH PUMPKIN, PROSCIUTTO & CHÈVRE

This is a great way to make sandwiches for a lot of people, and using giant rounds of focaccia (olive focaccia works really well here) means you can make 8 sandwiches at one time, super fast. We don't give measurements here, so make it as generous (or skimpy!) as you like. Pumpkin adds an earthy flavour to this incredible sandwich.

MAKES 8 SERVINGS

1 large focaccia (about 12 inches in diameter)

Canned unsweetened pumpkin purée

Chèvre (goat cheese)

Prosciutto

Avocado, sliced

Tomato or roasted bell pepper, sliced

Lettuce or sprouts

Slice the focaccia into two rounds. Spread one round with the pumpkin and the other with the chèvre. On the bottom round, layer prosciutto, avocado, tomato or roasted red pepper, and lettuce or sprouts. Sandwich with the top round. Using a sharp bread knife, slice the round into 8 even wedges, like a pizza.

LETTUCE WRAPS WITH SQUASH "NOODLES" & SPICY BEEF

An artful array of crisp, colourful veggies is visually stunning, and the "DIY" approach lets everyone get exactly what they want. Instead of glass noodles, we use spaghetti squash—it really soaks up the flavours of our Thai marinade and adds great texture.   MAKES ABOUT 12 WRAPS

Squash "Noodles"

1 teaspoon sweet chili sauce

½ teaspoon granulated sugar

Zest of 1 lime

Juice of ½ lime

½ clove garlic, minced

½ teaspoon chopped fresh gingerroot

1 tablespoon oil (any mild-tasting oil will do: peanut, sunflower or vegetable)

½ roasted spaghetti squash, forked into "noodles" (see page 24)

Spicy Beef

½ teaspoon Thai chili sauce (such as Sriracha)

1 teaspoon soy sauce

1 teaspoon granulated sugar

1 tablespoon oil (any mild-tasting oil will do here, peanut, sunflower, canola or vegetable)

1 flank steak (8 oz)

Garnishes

Bean sprouts

Crispy fresh veggies, chopped: carrot, daikon, red bell pepper and cucumber

Fresh cilantro, chopped

Fresh mint, chopped

Green onions, chopped

Roasted unsalted peanuts, chopped

1 to 2 heads red or green leaf lettuce

Make the noodles: In a large bowl, whisk together the chili sauce, sugar, lime zest and juice, garlic, ginger and oil. Add the spaghetti squash and toss to coat well. Set aside to marinate.

Make the spicy beef: In a bowl, whisk together the chili sauce, soy sauce and sugar and set aside.

In a frying pan, heat the oil over medium-high heat. Pan-fry the steak to medium-rare, 3 to 5 minutes per side (depending on thickness), and remove from the heat. Brush with the prepared sauce while the meat is still hot. Let rest for 3 minutes before slicing against the grain into strips.

To serve, arrange the garnishes in bowls at the centre of the serving table with a basket of lettuce leaves, the bowl of "noodles" and platter of steak.

BACON-WRAPPED BUTTERNUT STUFFED WITH KALE & BLUE CHEESE

Look for a butternut with a large base. The bigger the bowl, the more stuffing you can get into it. Not only is this dish literally stuffed with goodness, it is beautifully presented—and it has bacon. What are you waiting for?

MAKES 4 SERVINGS

1 butternut squash
1 tablespoon olive oil
Kosher salt and fresh cracked black
    pepper
2 slices bacon
1 tablespoon butter
¼ cup chopped onion

½ clove garlic, minced
1½ cups trimmed and chopped kale
    (centre rib removed)
2 slices rye, multigrain or sourdough
    bread
1½ tablespoons crumbled blue cheese

Preheat the oven to 375°F. Line a baking sheet with parchment paper.

Cut the round "bowl" end from the squash (reserve the "arm" for another use). Peel squash and discard the seeds. Brush squash all over with oil and season with salt and pepper. Place the squash cut-side down on the prepared baking sheet. Drape the bacon over the squash, crossing at right angles to form an X. Roast in preheated oven for 30 minutes, basting occasionally with bacon drippings. Remove from the oven and set aside.

Meanwhile, prepare the stuffing: In a large frying pan, melt the butter over medium-high heat. Sauté the onion and garlic until softened, about 1½ minutes. Stir in the kale and sauté for another 5 minutes. Remove from the heat and set aside.

Toast the bread and cut into ½-inch cubes. Gently stir into the kale mixture. Add the blue cheese and toss to combine.

Increase the oven temperature to 500°F. Turn the bacon-wrapped squash cut-side up on the baking sheet and tuck the dangling ends of bacon into the "bowl." Stuff to overflowing with the kale mixture. Bake for about 7 minutes. Remove from the oven and let cool for about 10 minutes before serving.

To serve, cut between the bacon slices.

SQUASH, PROSCIUTTO & PESTO PITA PIZZA

Pumpkin isn't often found on pizza, but its warm, nutty flavour goes beautifully with the prosciutto, bocconcini and pesto. While Rob makes his own pesto (see Tip) using the basil in his garden, you can just as easily grab a jar of pesto at the supermarket for this recipe. MAKES 1 PIZZA

1 pita bread (not pocket style)
2 tablespoons basil pesto (store-bought is fine)
2 slices prosciutto, torn into pieces
¼ cup bocconcini, sliced

½ cup roasted acorn squash (see pages 25–26), pulled into pieces
Kosher salt and fresh cracked black pepper
Freshly shaved Parmesan cheese

Preheat the oven to 350°F.

Toast the pita in preheated oven for 5 to 10 minutes or until browned and beginning to crisp up. Remove from the oven and, while still warm, spread with the pesto and top with the prosciutto, bocconcini and squash. Season with a pinch of salt and pepper. Bake for 3 to 5 minutes, until the bocconcini softens. Sprinkle with Parmesan before serving.

Tip: If you make homemade pesto, make extra and freeze it in smaller portions in ice-cube trays. Turn out frozen cubes into freezer bags. Then you can grab a shot of summery basil all year round (defrosting the cubes as needed).

TANDOORI MASALA SQUASH WITH RED RICE & BABY PEAS

Tandoori masala is a mixture of spices used in the traditional dishes of Northern India, Pakistan and Afghanistan. We've created a vegetarian version of classic chicken tikka masala by subbing in butternut squash for the chicken. We like to serve this with red cargo rice, a long-grain Thai rice somewhat similar to brown rice that is slightly sweet with a chewy texture, but of course you can use any rice that you have on hand.

MAKES 4 SERVINGS

½ cup red cargo rice

2 tablespoons olive oil

1 onion, diced

2 cups peeled cubed (1 inch) butternut squash

2 teaspoons tandoori masala (see Tip)

1 can (14 oz) coconut milk

1 teaspoon kosher salt

1 clove garlic, minced

1 fresh green chile, minced

Naan bread

1 cup frozen baby peas

½ cup plain yogurt

1 teaspoon pomegranate molasses

1 mango, peeled, pitted and chopped

Chopped fresh cilantro leaves, to taste

In a saucepan of boiling water, cook the rice until tender, about 30 minutes. Drain and cover to keep warm. Set aside.

Meanwhile, in a frying pan, heat the oil over medium-high heat. Add the onion, squash and tandoori masala and sauté until browned, about 3 minutes. Add the coconut milk, salt, garlic and chile and stir gently to combine. Reduce the heat to medium-low and cook for 20 minutes, stirring occasionally.

While the masala is cooking, prepare the naan, peas and garnishes: Warm the naan in a low oven. Steam or boil the peas, place in a bowl and set aside. Combine the yogurt and pomegranate molasses in a bowl and set aside. Combine the mango and cilantro in a bowl and set aside.

To serve, divide the cooked rice among the serving plates and ladle the tandoori squash overtop. Top each with the mango-cilantro mixture and drizzle with pomegranate yogurt. Serve with the warm naan bread and baby peas.

Tip: The best tandoori masala we've had is Arvinda's, which you can purchase online. Use whichever brand you prefer. To keep its potency, store it in the freezer, not your cupboard—it makes a big difference in flavour.

GLUTEN-FREE ZUCCHINI LASAGNA

Ivy was skeptical about this recipe at first: lasagna made with zucchini "noodles" instead of pasta? She worried that the zucchini would become soggy by the time the dish cooked, but the zucchini stays firm and green—a delicious alternative to pasta. We use ground pork in this dish, as beef is a bit too heavy and will overpower the zucchini. You could also use ground turkey or crumbled medium-firm tofu. If you are in a rush, you can substitute a jar (28 oz) of store-bought tomato sauce for the tomatoes, tomato paste, onion, celery and garlic. MAKES 6 SERVINGS

1 tablespoon olive oil
1 onion, chopped
2 ribs celery, chopped
2 cloves garlic, minced
1 can (5½ oz) tomato paste
1 can (28 oz) crushed tomatoes,
   with juice
½ pound medium ground pork

1 tablespoon soy sauce
Kosher salt and fresh cracked black
   pepper
2 medium zucchini, sliced lengthwise
   ⅛-inch thick
1 cup shredded mozzarella cheese
Grated Parmesan cheese

In a large saucepan, heat the oil over medium-high heat. Sauté the onion, celery and garlic for 2 to 3 minutes, until fragrant. Stir in the tomato paste and tomatoes. Bring to a simmer and add the pork, stirring well to break up the pieces. Stir in the soy sauce. Cover the pan, reduce the heat, and simmer for 20 minutes, until pork is cooked through. Season with salt and pepper to taste.

Preheat the oven to 375°F. Grease an 8- × 8-inch square baking pan with oil.

Assemble the lasagna: Spoon a little meat sauce into the bottom of the prepared pan and spread it around. Arrange some zucchini slices in a single layer to completely cover the bottom of the pan. Spread 1 cup meat sauce evenly overtop and sprinkle with ¼ cup mozzarella. Follow with another layer of zucchini, meat sauce and mozzarella. Repeat the layers one more time, finishing with a layer of zucchini. Sprinkle with the remaining mozzarella and grate some Parmesan overtop (can be made up to here and refrigerated a day in advance).

Bake, uncovered, in preheated oven for 30 to 40 minutes, or until the sauce is bubbling around the sides. Remove from the oven and let sit for 20 minutes before serving (this will help the lasagna "set" and make it easier to slice).

FISH CAKES & ZUCCHINI SALAD

Smoked fish, whether trout, sturgeon or mackerel, can be a lovely appetizer served on its own, or you can transform it into these marvellous fish cakes, which are crispy on the outside and soft and moist on the inside. Served over a simple zucchini salad, an appetizer-sized amount of smoked fish is easily stretched into a dinner for five.

MAKES 4 TO 5 FISH CAKES

Fish Cakes

2 cups flaked smoked trout, mackerel or
  other fish

1 tablespoon capers, drained and
  chopped

1 teaspoon hot sauce (or more to taste)

¼ cup finely chopped red bell pepper

2 green onions, white and green parts,
  finely chopped

1 tablespoon Dijon mustard

2 tablespoons mayonnaise

1½ cups mashed roasted butternut or
  acorn squash (see page 26)

1½ cups mashed potatoes

Kosher salt and fresh cracked black pepper

1 cup dried breadcrumbs or panko breadcrumbs

1 egg

Pinch of cayenne (optional)

Zucchini Salad

1 zucchini, peeled into ribbons (see page
  23)

1 bunch of watercress, stemmed

Honey-Cider Vinaigrette (page 138)

Make the fish cakes: In a food processor fitted with the metal blade, pulse the smoked fish just until crumbled (be careful not to over-process; you want the fish cakes to have some texture). Transfer the fish to a large bowl. Add the capers, hot sauce, red pepper, green onions, Dijon mustard, mayonnaise, squash and potato and stir well to combine. Finely dice 2 to 3 strips of zucchini and stir into the mixture. Season with salt and pepper to taste, then stir in the egg until well combined. Using your hands, form the mixture into 4 or 5 patties. Cover and set aside in the refrigerator.

Prepare your breading station: In one bowl, combine the breadcrumbs and salt and pepper to taste (if you like, add a pinch of cayenne for some kick). In another bowl, beat the egg.

Dredge the fish patties in the breadcrumbs and dust off the excess, then dip them in the egg wash and end with a final coating of breadcrumbs. Cover and refrigerate.

In a frying pan, heat ¼ inch oil over medium-high heat (when a drop of water sizzles in the pan, it is hot enough). Cook the patties (be careful not to crowd the pan; you may have to cook these in batches) for 3 to 5 minutes each side, until golden brown. Keep warm in a low oven until all patties are fried and warmed through.

Make the salad: Meanwhile, toss the watercress and zucchini in a bowl with the vinaigrette.

To serve, make a bed of salad on each serving plate and top with one or two fish cakes. Garnish with salsa or tartar sauce and a lemon wedge alongside.

GRILLED ZUCCHINI & HALIBUT KEBABS

If you're a little nervous about grilling, Rob recommends this recipe to start with: it cooks quickly and doesn't require a lot of expertise.

MAKES 8 NINE-INCH KEBABS

1 pound halibut, cut into 1-inch cubes
Kosher salt and fresh cracked black
   pepper
Extra virgin olive oil

1 to 2 zucchini, cut into ½-inch-thick
   rounds
Lemon wedges
Butternut Chutney (page 151)

Preheat the grill to medium-high.

Season the halibut with salt and pepper and drizzle lightly with oil. Leave the zucchini plain (you'll be jazzing it up after the grilling).

Thread the skewers (see Tip) with alternating pieces of zucchini (skewer through the outside edge of the rounds so that the flesh is in contact with the grill) and halibut, leaving space at both ends for grabbing.

Grill for about 2 minutes, until grill marks appear on one side, then turn and grill the other side for another 2 minutes, until the fish is cooked through (the fish should be opaque and feel firm to the touch). Transfer to a platter and season with additional salt and pepper. Drizzle with your best olive oil. Serve with lemon wedges and Butternut Chutney alongside.

Tip: You can use metal skewers or wooden ones. Soak wooden skewers in water for 20 to 30 minutes before using them, to reduce the chances of their burning on the grill.

FISH & OLD BAY SQUASH CHIPS

Our version of this classic features oven-baked breaded whitefish served alongside Old Bay–seasoned squash "chips." Ivy first discovered Old Bay seasoning while working on Lynn Crawford's Food Network show Pitchin' In, and she's been a fan of the spice blend ever since. Although cooking breaded fish or chicken in the oven is healthier than frying it, it often makes for a lacklustre crust, so we like to use Japanese-style panko breadcrumbs for a crispy, airy coating.　　　**MAKES 4 SERVINGS**

Chips
1 hubbard squash, cut into french fries
2 tablespoons Old Bay seasoning (see Tip)

Fish
1 cup panko breadcrumbs
1 egg
¼ cup all-purpose flour

Kosher salt and fresh cracked black pepper
4 skin-on whitefish filets

Garnishes
Tartar sauce
Lemon wedges
Malt vinegar

Preheat the oven to 400°F. Line 2 baking sheets with parchment paper (one for the chips, the other for the fish).

In a large bowl, toss the squash with the Old Bay seasoning until evenly coated. Arrange the squash in a single layer on a parchment-lined baking sheet. Bake in preheated oven for 15 minutes.

Meanwhile, prepare your breading station: Place the panko on a microwave-safe dish and heat for 1 to 2 minutes, stirring every 30 seconds, until the desired brownness is achieved. (Alternatively, you can cook the panko in a dry frying pan over medium heat, stirring constantly, until it browns, about 5 minutes.) Beat the egg in a shallow dish. Place the flour in another shallow dish, season with a pinch of salt and pepper and stir to combine.

Dredge both sides of the fish in the flour, then dip in the egg, and then coat with the browned panko. Place the fish on the prepared baking sheet and transfer to the oven to cook with the chips.

Once the chips have browned on one side, remove the sheet from the oven, turn the chips over and return to the oven along with the fish. Bake for another 15 minutes, or until the chips are golden brown and the fish is cooked through. Serve immediately with tartar sauce, lemon wedges and malt vinegar.

Tip: Old Bay seasoning is a blend of 18 herbs and spices. You can make a substitute by mixing equal amounts celery salt, paprika and hot pepper flakes.

SPAGHETTI PIE

Kerry wanted to create a dish that his nephews and nieces would enjoy, something whimsical and fun where they wouldn't be scared away by the squash. So he took spaghetti squash and used it as a pie crust. Kids love this dish. It's spaghetti, and it's pie. It's healthy, delicious and fun. Hello!

MAKES 1 NINE-INCH PIE

1 medium roasted spaghetti squash, forked into "noodles" (see page 24)

1 egg

3 tablespoons all-purpose flour

1 teaspoon baking powder

1 teaspoon kosher salt

1 teaspoon fresh cracked black pepper

3 cups very thick Bolognese sauce (store-bought is fine)

2 tablespoons grated Parmesan cheese

Preheat the oven to 350°F. Grease a 9-inch pie plate.

In a bowl, combine the squash and egg. Add the flour, baking powder, salt and pepper and stir until just combined. Gently press the mixture into the prepared pie plate to form the "pie shell." Bake in preheated oven for 30 minutes.

Meanwhile, warm the Bolognese sauce in a saucepan over low heat.

Remove the "pie shell" from the oven and fill with warmed Bolognese sauce. Sprinkle evenly with Parmesan. Serve immediately.

CAULIFLOWER & SQUASH WITH CREAMY EGG NOODLES

If you have your cauliflower and squash prepped in advance, this dish comes together very quickly. We like to serve it with the Marinated Squash & Chayote Salad with Avocado & Melon (page 130).

MAKES 4 SERVINGS

1 package (12 oz) dried egg noodles

2 tablespoons butter

½ cup minced onion

2 tablespoons all-purpose flour

1 tablespoon horseradish (optional)

1 cup plain yogurt

1 cup sour cream

2 cups cauliflower florets, steamed

1 cup roasted spaghetti squash, forked into "noodles" (see page 24)

2 teaspoons paprika (hot or sweet, to taste)

Kosher salt and fresh cracked black pepper

1 tablespoon poppy seeds (optional)

Chopped fresh chives and dill, for garnish

In a pot of boiling salted water, cook egg noodles according to the package instructions. Drain and transfer to a large serving bowl.

Meanwhile, in a saucepan, melt the butter over medium heat. Sauté the onion until it begins to soften, about 1½ minutes. Sprinkle in the flour and cook, stirring, for about 2 minutes. (Reduce the heat if the onion starts to brown too quickly.) Stir in the horseradish (if using), yogurt and sour cream. Reduce the heat to low and cook, stirring often, for 5 minutes. Stir in the cauliflower and squash and heat through. Add the paprika and salt and pepper to taste.

Pour the veggie sauce over the egg noodles. Sprinkle with the poppy seeds (if using), chives and dill. Toss and serve immediately.

CHICKEN BREASTS STUFFED WITH SPINACH & PUMPKIN

Don't be intimidated by stuffing something other than a whole chicken. Puréed pumpkin is the perfect consistency for tucking under chicken skin and stays in place while cooking. This recipe usually makes enough for four people, especially if you use chicken supremes, or suprême de volaire, a skin-on chicken breast with the wing bone (drumette) attached. If you add potatoes to the pan after the first 10 minutes of cooking, you'll have an easy one-dish meal (see Tip). **MAKES 4 SERVINGS**

3 tablespoons butter, divided

½ onion, chopped

1 clove garlic, chopped

1 cup packed baby spinach leaves

1 egg

⅓ cup canned unsweetened pumpkin purée

¼ teaspoon kosher salt

¼ teaspoon fresh cracked black pepper

½ teaspoon ground nutmeg

⅓ cup grated Parmesan cheese

1 teaspoon soy sauce

2 large skin-on chicken breast supremes

Preheat the oven to 400°F. Grease a baking dish.

Make the stuffing: In a frying pan, melt 2 tablespoons butter over medium heat. Sauté the onion and garlic until softened, about 1½ minutes. Add the spinach and cook, stirring constantly, just until the spinach wilts. Remove from the heat and set aside.

In a separate bowl, combine the egg, pumpkin, salt, pepper and nutmeg. Stir in the Parmesan and cooked spinach mixture. Set aside.

Make the glaze: In a small saucepan, melt the remaining 1 tablespoon of butter over medium heat. Stir in the soy sauce. Remove from heat and set aside.

Stuff the chicken: Using your fingers, carefully part the breast skin from the breast meat, forming a pocket. Carefully stuff half of the squash and spinach mixture between the skin and meat of each breast. Place breasts side by side in prepared baking dish. Brush with the butter and soy sauce glaze. Roast in preheated oven for 40 minutes, basting with juices at the 10-minute and 30-minute marks, until the skin is crispy. Remove from the oven and set aside for 5 minutes to rest. Slice the chicken breast for serving.

Tip: This dish goes really well with roasted potatoes. Just add quartered potatoes to the baking dish alongside the chicken at the 10-minute mark, basting them with the chicken juices.

NO-MESS BAKED RIGATONI WITH SAUSAGE, BUTTERNUT & TOMATO

A hearty baked pasta bursting with sweet butternut squash and robust Italian sausage and topped with melty mozzarella, this is an easy one-dish dinner that's hard to ignore. Our trick of lining the baking dish with parchment paper before adding the pasta makes cleaning up a cinch, too!

MAKES 4 SERVINGS

½ pound dried rigatoni pasta

2 large Italian pork sausages (uncooked), cut into 1-inch pieces (about 2 cups)

1 cup roasted cubed butternut squash (see page 25)

2½ cups tomato sauce (store-bought is fine)

1 teaspoon kosher salt

1 teaspoon fresh cracked black pepper

2 cups shredded mozzarella cheese

Preheat the oven to 350°F. Line a 9- × 13-inch baking dish or large casserole dish with parchment paper. **Cook** the pasta in a pot of boiling salted water until just before al dente, 5 to 7 minutes (it will finish cooking in the oven). Drain well.

In a large bowl, combine the sausage, squash and tomato sauce. Stir in the pasta. Season with the salt and pepper, stirring well to combine. Pour into the prepared baking dish and sprinkle evenly with the cheese. Cover with foil and bake for 50 minutes. Remove the foil and bake for 5 minutes longer, until golden brown. Let rest for 10 minutes before serving.

ROAST CHICKEN STUFFED WITH SQUASH & WILD RICE

This is not your everyday stuffed chicken, but our take on this family classic may just become your favourite. Sage, commonly used in traditional stuffing, lends a familiar note to the nutty wild rice and sweet, succulent squash.

MAKES 6 SERVINGS

2 cups lightly packed torn white bread (about 2 slices)

1 cup cooked wild rice

1 cup mashed roasted butternut or acorn squash (see page 26)

2 teaspoons chopped fresh sage leaves or savory

Kosher salt and fresh cracked black pepper

1 teaspoon olive oil

½ white onion, finely diced

1 to 2 tablespoons water

1 whole chicken (3½ to 4 pounds)

1 tablespoon butter, softened

½ teaspoon kosher salt

½ teaspoon fresh cracked black pepper

Preheat the oven to 450°F.

In a bowl, combine the bread, rice, squash and sage leaves and season with salt and pepper to taste.

In a frying pan, heat the oil over medium heat. Sauté the onion for 1½ minutes, until softened, and add to the bread mixture. Add the water and, using your hands, thoroughly combine.

Stuff the rice and squash mixture into the chicken (see Tip). Truss the drumstick ends together using butcher's twine. Rub the chicken all over with the butter, season generously with the salt and pepper and place on a roasting rack in a roasting pan. Roast for 15 minutes in preheated oven, then reduce the heat to 375°F and roast for about 75 minutes, basting the bird twice while cooking. If you like, you can add parsnips, carrots and potatoes under the rack in the roasting pan at the 40-minute mark.

Tip: Using a wide-mouthed canning funnel to stuff the bird makes the job much neater and more efficient. You can find one in most dollar stores or kitchen supply stores.

SWEDISH MEATBALLS WITH SQUASH & MUSHROOM STROGANOFF

Chef Alexandra Feswick of Toronto's Drake Hotel shared this recipe with us after we tried her version at Terroir, Canada's largest annual food symposium. Tender meatballs, sweet squash and earthy mushrooms coated in a rich sauce make for a hearty and warming meal on a chilly evening. Her secret? A pinch of cardamom. It sounds crazy but just give it a try. Serve over brown rice or egg noodles, garnished with a little chopped parsley. MAKES 4 SERVINGS

½ pound medium ground beef

½ pound medium ground pork

Kosher salt and fresh cracked black pepper

½ onion, chopped

2 large button or cremini mushrooms, chopped

2 cups peeled chopped butternut squash

2 tablespoons butter

2 tablespoons all-purpose flour

1 can (14 oz) chicken stock

½ cup whipping (35%) cream

½ cup sour cream

Pinch of ground cardamom

1 teaspoon soy sauce

¼ teaspoon ground allspice

Chopped fresh parsley leaves, for garnish (optional)

In a bowl, combine the beef and pork and season with salt and pepper to taste. Using the palm of your hands, form meatballs (we make ours golf ball–size).

In a large, oiled saucepan over medium heat, cook the meatballs in batches until browned all over. Transfer the cooked meatballs to a plate.

Drain all but 1 tablespoon fat from the pan. Sauté the onion until softened, about 1½ minutes. Add the mushrooms and squash and stir to combine. Stir in the butter and flour. Cook, stirring constantly, for 1 to 2 minutes, until the flour darkens. Stir in the chicken stock, then the cream and sour cream. Add the cardamom, soy sauce and allspice and stir well. Taste and adjust the seasoning with salt and pepper, if needed. Return the cooked meatballs to the pan, gently stir to combine and cook for about 5 minutes, until the squash is cooked through. If the mixture is too thick, add a splash of water or milk. Serve immediately, sprinkled with chopped parsley, if desired.

OSSO BUCO WITH BUTTERNUT & CANNELLINI MASH

Osso buco is Italian for "bone with a hole," a description of the veal shank used in the dish. It is often served with risotto, but it matches beautifully with a creamy side of savoury butternut squash mashed with cannellini beans and a touch of fresh thyme.   MAKES 6 SERVINGS

Osso Buco

4 veal shanks of similar size
   (6 to 8 oz each)
Kosher salt and fresh cracked black
   pepper
1 tablespoon olive oil
1 small onion, sliced
2 ribs celery, diced
1 large clove garlic, minced
1 cup red wine (see Tip)

1 cup beef stock (see headnote, page 68)
2 bay leaves

White Bean Mash

2 cups mashed roasted butternut squash
   (see page 26)
1 can (14 oz) cannellini beans, rinsed
   and drained
3 to 5 sprigs fresh thyme
⅓ cup table (18%) cream or milk
1 tablespoon butter

Make the osso buco: Preheat the oven to 325°F. Season the shanks with salt and pepper to taste.
In a heavy-bottomed frying pan over medium-high heat, heat the oil until shimmery. Sear the shanks for 2 to 3 minutes per side, just to brown (not to cook through), then transfer to a plate and set aside.
To the pan, add the onion and celery and cook, stirring constantly, for 1½ minutes, until softened, then stir in the garlic. Add the red wine and stock. Return the shanks to the pan and add the bay leaves. Cover with a tight-fitting lid and bake in preheated oven for 2 hours, or until meltingly tender.
Make the cannellini mash: Meanwhile, in a heavy-bottomed saucepan over medium-high heat, combine the squash, cannellini beans, thyme and cream and simmer for 2 to 3 minutes, until heated through. Purée the mixture in a food processor, then return the pan, cover and set aside.
Before serving, warm the mash, adding the butter. Stir well to combine and season with salt and pepper to taste.
To serve, scoop the mash into a shallow, wide-brimmed bowl. Top with osso buco and ladle the braising liquid overtop, or serve separately, as shown.

Tip: We don't believe in using expensive wine for cooking. As long as the wine has not gone off, cheap plonk will be just fine. (Keep your best wine for drinking.)

SAVOURY BUTTERCUP & SAUSAGE BAKE WITH CURRANTS

A one-pot wonder, this is a full-on, stick-to-your-ribs dinner inspired by the Mennonite farmers who live near Stratford, Ontario, and the Polish delis that line Roncesvalles Avenue near the Knights' home in Toronto. The flavours and traditions of Southwestern Ontario and Eastern Europe are combined in this hearty dish that is even better the next day, if you manage to have any leftovers.

MAKES 2 SERVINGS

1 tablespoon olive oil

1 pound of pork sausages (mild, not spicy)

2 onions, chopped

3 cups peeled cubed (1 inch) buttercup squash

Kosher salt and fresh cracked black pepper

1 tablespoon chopped fresh summer savory or sage leaves

1 tablespoon currants or golden raisins

Sour cream

Applesauce

Preheat the oven to 350°F.

In an oven-proof frying pan with a lid, heat the oil over medium-high heat. Cook the sausages until browned all over. Transfer to a plate and set aside.

Add the onions to the pan and sauté in the juices of the sausage until softened. Add the squash and stir to mix well. Place the browned sausage on top of the squash and onion mixture. Season with salt and pepper to taste and sprinkle with the savory and currants. Cover and bake in preheated oven for 25 minutes.

Serve warm with sour cream and applesauce alongside.

Friendly Fibre

Squash is high in fibre and relatively
low in sugar—another reason it is an excellent
part of a healthy diet. Winter squashes like acorn,
butternut and pumpkin have about one-third
of the recommended daily intake
of fibre in just one cup.

SALADS & SIDES

Squash is all too often found in the margins of a meal, shoved to the side and underappreciated. But we're here to tell you that squash can completely transform a simple salad or side dish into something really wonderful, with colour, great taste and an infusion of nutrients. Try these sides and salads and you may find that dishes with squash will be the first thing to disappear from the table.

Clockwise from top left: Zippy Zucchini Refrigerator Pickles (page 168); Spaghetti Squash Puttanesca (page 166); Cheesy Baked Acorn Squash & Cauliflower Casserole (page 156); Kabocha Devilled Eggs (page 127); and Diner Wedge Salad with Yogurt Ranch Dressing (page 132).

SWEET & SPICY PUMPKIN SEEDS

Carving pumpkins may not be good for making pies, but their seeds make a delicious and healthy snack that's easy to prepare while you put the finishing touches on your jack-o'-lanterns.

MAKES 1 CUP

1 cup pumpkin seeds

1 tablespoon olive oil

1 tablespoon lightly packed brown sugar

½ teaspoon ground cinnamon

¼ teaspoon ground nutmeg

¼ teaspoon chili powder

½ teaspoon kosher salt

½ teaspoon fresh cracked black pepper

Preheat the oven to 300°F. Line a baking sheet with parchment paper or foil.

Cut a lid in your pumpkin and scoop out the gloopy seeds. Place the seeds in a colander and give them a rinse under cold running water. Spread the seeds out on paper towels and pat dry. You will have some slimy strands still clinging to the seeds, but don't worry: they will cook up just fine. Measure out 1 cup pumpkin seeds.

In a large bowl, combine the oil, brown sugar, cinnamon, nutmeg, chili powder, salt and pepper. Add the pumpkin seeds and mix thoroughly.

Spread the seeds evenly over the prepared baking sheet. Bake in preheated oven for about 45 minutes, stirring every 15 minutes, until the seeds are slightly browned on both sides. Remove from the oven and cool slightly before serving.

KABOCHA DEVILLED EGGS

Mashed kabocha adds a delicate nutty flavour and bright golden colour to the yolk mixture of these devilled eggs, not to mention nutritional benefits. It also adds lightness and volume, so you won't run out of stuffing. You might never make devilled eggs the old way again. (Photo on pages 122–124.)

MAKES 14 PIECES

7 eggs
½ cup mashed roasted kabocha, acorn or butternut squash (see page 26)
½ green onion, white and green parts, chopped
1 teaspoon Dijon mustard

2 tablespoons mayonnaise
Kosher salt and fresh cracked black pepper
1 teaspoon chopped mixed fresh herbs (thyme, chives or parsley; optional)
Pinch of hot paprika

Place the eggs in a saucepan with enough cold water to cover them by an inch. Set the timer for 18 minutes. Bring to a simmer, uncovered, over high heat. Eggs are easier to peel when they are cooled down quickly, so set up a bowl of ice water in your sink. When the timer goes off, use a slotted spoon to scoop the eggs into the prepared ice bath.

Once cooled, peel the eggs and cut in half. Separate the cooked yolks from the whites and transfer the yolks to a bowl. Arrange the halved whites on a platter that's been lined with a napkin or paper towel (to keep them from sliding all over).

In a food processor fitted with the metal blade, blitz the yolks, squash, green onion, Dijon mustard and mayonnaise until smooth. (Alternatively, you can mash them using a fork.) Season with salt and pepper to taste.

Fill the egg whites with generous spoonfuls of the filling. Sprinkle with chopped fresh herbs (if using) and a dusting of paprika. Chill well before serving.

RICOTTA-STUFFED
ZUCCHINI BLOSSOMS

The zucchini flowers in this recipe are basically a pretty delivery vessel for the delicious ricotta stuffing. To keep it on the healthy side, Kerry bakes rather than deep-fries them. Browning the breadcrumbs before coating the blossoms ensures a beautifully toasted, golden crust. The mild, herbaceous flavour of the blossoms infuses the creamy ricotta and tastes like springtime. MAKES 10 BLOSSOMS

1½ cups extra-smooth ricotta

2 tablespoons chopped fresh herbs (parsley, dill, thyme or a combo of all three)

½ teaspoon Dijon mustard

Zest of ½ orange

Zest of ½ lemon

Fresh lemon juice

Kosher salt and fresh cracked black pepper

10 medium zucchini blossoms (about 2 inches in length)

2 eggs

2 cups panko breadcrumbs or dried breadcrumbs

In a bowl, combine the ricotta, herbs, Dijon mustard, orange and lemon zests and lemon juice. Season with salt and pepper to taste.

Gently open the blossoms and spoon the ricotta mixture inside, filling them almost to the top. (Alternatively, pipe it in using a piping bag or resealable bag with the tip snipped off.) Gently twist the blossom ends to seal. Place the filled blossoms on a parchment-lined baking sheet and chill in the refrigerator for at least 20 minutes.

While the blossoms chill, preheat the oven to 400°F.

Make your toasted, golden crumbs: Place the breadcrumbs in a microwave-safe dish and cook for 30 seconds. Stir well and microwave for another 30 seconds. Repeat until the breadcrumbs turn nicely golden. Set aside to cool. Alternatively, toast in a dry frying pan over medium-high heat, stirring constantly, until golden brown.

Prepare your breading station: In one bowl, beat the eggs. In another, place the cooled breadcrumbs.

Dip each blossom first in the beaten egg, then in the breadcrumbs, tapping off the excess. Then dip in the egg again and finish with another coating of breadcrumbs (so each blossom is double-dipped). Place the stuffed blossoms on the prepared baking sheet and bake in preheated oven for 10 minutes, until browned and crispy. Serve immediately.

Tip: You'll find zucchini blossoms in farmers' markets and specialty grocery stores from late spring through early summer.

MARINATED SQUASH & CHAYOTE SALAD WITH AVOCADO & MELON

This salad is beautiful when all the ingredients are in hues of green, using zucchini and honeydew melon, or you can add a touch of yellow with crookneck or summer squash and some peachy orange with cantaloupe. It's up to you. Feel free to add some herbs to the dressing—a little sprinkle of picked chervil or tarragon is lovely with this (or chive flowers—beautiful!). **MAKES 2 SERVINGS**

2 tablespoons liquid honey

2 tablespoons olive oil

Juice of 1 lemon

Kosher salt and fresh cracked black pepper

1 crookneck squash or zucchini, peeled into ribbons (see page 23)

½ chayote squash, thinly sliced (see Tip)

1 ripe avocado, pitted, peeled and sliced into thin vertical wedges

¼ ripe melon, peeled, seeded and sliced into horizontal wedges

Kosher salt and fresh cracked black pepper

Chopped fresh herbs (chives, parsley, tarragon or chervil), for garnish

In a large bowl, whisk together the honey, oil and lemon juice and season with salt and pepper to taste. Toss the squashes with the dressing and marinate for 20 to 30 minutes in the refrigerator. **Divide** the salad among serving plates and top with the avocado and melon. Season lightly with salt and pepper, sprinkle with herbs and drizzle with any dressing left in the bowl. Serve immediately.

Tip: A mandolin makes slicing squash thinly a cinch. You can find inexpensive plastic models at most kitchen supply stores. If you don't have one handy, a Y-shaped speed peeler will do.

DINER WEDGE SALAD WITH YOGURT RANCH DRESSING

This salad is all about the dressing, which is inspired by the homemade ranch dressing made by Ivy's friend and one of her favourite chefs, Anthony Rose, of Rose & Sons in Toronto. Even if you sneak tofu and lima beans into the mix, your family will still be lapping it up and asking for seconds. (Photo on pages 122–124.)

MAKES 6 SERVINGS

Dressing
½ cup plain yogurt
1 teaspoon fresh lemon juice
1 teaspoon red wine vinegar
1½ teaspoons liquid honey
1 teaspoon hot sauce (or to taste, just enough to get a tiny bit of heat)
½ green onion, white and green parts, chopped
1 sprig of fresh thyme, chopped

Salad
1 head iceberg lettuce, cut into 6 wedges
½ cup roasted cubed acorn squash (see page 25)
20 cherry tomatoes, halved
1 avocado, pitted, peeled and cut into ½-inch cubes
1 cucumber, thinly sliced
1 red onion, thinly sliced
1 red or yellow bell pepper, seeded and sliced

Garnishes (optional)
Crumbled crispy bacon
Crumbled blue cheese

Make the dressing: Combine all of the dressing ingredients in a jar, seal tightly and shake well. If the dressing seems too thick, add 1 teaspoon water. Refrigerate until ready to use (will keep for up to 4 days).

Make the salad: Place each wedge of lettuce in a serving bowl, flattening it out a bit to separate the leaves. Top with squash, tomatoes, avocado, cucumber, onion and red pepper. Spoon the dressing overtop. Finish with some bacon and blue cheese (if using).

AVOCADO, SQUASH & BACON SALAD WITH EASIEST-EVER VINAIGRETTE

Sometimes the simplest solutions are the best: "I wanted something simple, bright and light to counteract the richness of the avocado, bacon and roasted squash," explains Ivy. "But I was in a rush and didn't want to concoct a 'recipe' for a dressing, so I ignored the whisk, the jar and the mixing bowl and just threw some red wine vinegar and nice olive oil on top of the salad fixings. Toss and serve. It's that simple." This salad is a visual stunner because all the components are green except for the golden nuggets of squash and the crispy bacon—making it easier to spot the bacon in your bowl, which is always a bonus. MAKES 4 SERVINGS

2 ripe avocados (see Tip)

1 cucumber, sliced

1 small zucchini, peeled into ribbons (see page 23)

6 strips crispy bacon

1 cup roasted cubed butternut squash (see page 25)

1 head leaf lettuce, torn into bite-sized pieces

1 tablespoon red wine vinegar

2 tablespoons extra virgin olive oil

Kosher salt and fresh cracked black pepper

¼ cup roasted unsalted sunflower seeds

1 green onion, white and green parts, chopped

In a large serving bowl, toss together the avocados, cucumber, zucchini, bacon, squash and lettuce. Drizzle with the vinegar and oil. Season with salt and pepper to taste. Toss gently. Serve garnished with a sprinkling of sunflower seeds and green onion.

Tip: To check that an avocado is ripe but not past its prime, gently squeeze it, making sure that there are no hollow spaces between the skin and the flesh, and that the flesh is only slightly soft, offering the same resistance as your flattened palm. If the stem nub is still attached, gently pop it off with your thumb: if the space underneath is green, the fruit is not overripe.

ZUCCHINI, CLEMENTINE & EDAMAME SALAD WITH HERBED FETA DRESSING

Zucchini and clementines are an unexpected combination, but they work together beautifully, especially when tossed with herbed feta dressing. **MAKES 2 MAIN-COURSE SALADS**

Salad
1 zucchini, peeled into ribbons
    (see page 23)
½ cup frozen edamame, thawed (see Tip)
1 clementine, peeled and separated into
    segments
A few handfuls of alfalfa sprouts

Dressing
2 tablespoons extra virgin olive oil
2 tablespoons crumbled feta
1 tablespoon chopped fresh chives
1 teaspoon white wine vinegar
½ teaspoon liquid honey (or to taste)
½ teaspoon orange juice
Squeeze of fresh lemon juice
3 sprigs fresh thyme, chopped
Fresh cracked black pepper

Make the salad: In a large bowl combine the zucchini, edamame and clementine. Add the sprouts, pulling them apart so they don't stay in one big clump. Toss to combine.

Make the dressing: Combine all of the dressing ingredients in a jar, seal and shake to blend.

Pour the dressing over the salad and toss to coat evenly. Divide between salad plates and serve.

Tip: You can substitute an equal amount of fresh or frozen lima beans for the edamame, if desired.

SPINACH SALAD WITH ACORN RINGS & WARM BACON VINAIGRETTE

Cutting the acorn squash into rings makes for a unique presentation: the outer ridges give the rings a floral appearance. You'll find that the peel is thin enough that it doesn't need to be removed before eating.

MAKES 4 TO 6 SERVINGS

1 acorn squash
Kosher salt and fresh cracked black
   pepper
2 large handfuls of baby spinach leaves
4 strips bacon, cut into matchsticks

⅓ cup sliced red onion
⅓ cup chopped zucchini
1½ tablespoons red wine vinegar
2 teaspoons grainy mustard
2 tablespoons extra virgin olive oil

Preheat the oven to 450°F. Line a baking sheet with parchment paper and grease lightly.

Using the mallet technique shown on page 22, cut the acorn squash crosswise into 4 to 6 rings (it helps to first cut a small piece off one side to create a flat base, so the acorn squash is more stable when cutting). Scrape the seeds out of the rings using the snap lid from a Mason jar and discard.

Place the rings on the prepared baking sheet and season with salt and pepper to taste. Roast in preheated oven for 5 minutes. Remove from the oven and turn rings over. Reduce the heat to 350°F and roast for another 10 minutes, until tender. Using a small biscuit cutter or paring knife, cut the centre out of any rings that had no seeds (so all the rings look alike). Set aside.

Place the spinach in a large bowl and set aside.

In a frying pan over medium-high heat, cook the bacon until browned. Transfer the cooked bacon to a plate lined in paper towel, reserving the bacon fat in the pan. Add the onion and zucchini to the pan and cook for 4 to 6 minutes, until the zucchini is browned. Stir in the vinegar, mustard, oil and bacon. Pour the onion and zucchini mixture over the spinach, season with salt and pepper to taste and toss well to coat.

To serve, divide the salad among serving plates and top each with a circle of roasted acorn squash.

KALE SALAD WITH BUTTERNUT SQUASH, BLUE CHEESE & HONEY-CIDER VINAGRETTE

Kale is a robust leafy green, so it can stand up to the big flavours in this salad. The sweetness of the squash, complexity of the blue cheese and the tart zing of the pomegranate make an unforgettable combination. The flaxseed oil in the dressing rounds out the plethora of superfoods, making this a salad fit for an action hero.

MAKES 4 SERVINGS

Vinaigrette
2 tablespoons red wine vinegar
¼ cup sunflower oil
1 tablespoon apple cider (unsweetened)
1 tablespoon flaxseed oil
1 teaspoon Dijon mustard
1 teaspoon honey

Salad
3 cups trimmed and thinly sliced kale (centre rib removed)
1 cup roasted cubed butternut squash (see page 25)
¼ cup crumbled blue cheese
¼ cup pomegranate seeds

Make the vinaigrette: Combine all of the vinaigrette ingredients in a jar, seal with the lid and shake to combine. Set aside. (This recipe makes extra vinaigrette. Use it in other dishes, such as Zucchini Salad on page 100.)

Make the salad: In a large bowl, toss together the kale, squash and blue cheese. Toss with vinaigrette to taste (see Tip). Divide the salad among serving bowls and sprinkle with pomegranate seeds before serving.

Tip: You can toss this salad with the vinaigrette and serve it right away or refrigerate it overnight to allow the flavours to further meld and the kale to soften.

THREE SISTERS FRY UP

This recipe brings together three traditional staples of the Americas—squash, beans and corn, known as the "three sisters." When corn is in season, Rob will grill up as much as he can, slice the kernels off the cob and freeze them for that sweet roasted corn taste all year long. You can use frozen corn niblets here, of course, but nothing beats the flavour of grilled corn. Although this recipe calls for cannellini beans, it can be made with pinto, garbanzo, red kidney or black beans. MAKES 4 SERVINGS

2 teaspoons sunflower or vegetable oil

½ small onion, diced

2 cups roasted spaghetti squash, forked into "noodles" (see page 24)

1 cup corn kernels

1 can (14 oz) cannellini beans, rinsed and drained

1 teaspoon red wine vinegar

Heat the oil in a frying pan over medium-high heat. Sauté the onion until softened, about 1½ minutes, then add the squash, corn, beans and vinegar. Stir well and cook for 3 to 4 minutes until heated through.

PESTO PASTA SALAD

This pasta salad packs a whole whack of veggies into one dish. You toss it together while the pasta is still hot, and the residual heat releases the full flavours of the veggies, chèvre and pesto. Let it cool and pack it up for a picnic in the park.   MAKES 4 SERVINGS

1 cup roasted cubed butternut squash (see page 25)

2 handfuls of baby spinach leaves

1 red bell pepper, seeded and chopped

10 cherry tomatoes, sliced

2 cups dried whole-wheat fusilli pasta

⅓ cup chèvre (goat cheese)

2 tablespoons basil pesto (store-bought is fine)

½ cup raw pumpkin seeds

Kosher salt and fresh cracked black pepper

Extra virgin olive oil (optional)

Red wine vinegar (optional)

In a large bowl, combine the squash, spinach, red pepper and tomatoes and set aside.

In a pot of boiling salted water, cook the pasta according to the package instructions, until al dente. Drain well.

Add the hot pasta to the bowl of veggies and toss to combine. Add the chèvre and pesto and toss until everything is well coated. Sprinkle with the pumpkin seeds and season with salt and pepper to taste. Drizzle with oil and red wine vinegar, if you like, just a bit to add some moisture and zing. Chill before serving.

PULL-APART ACORN SALAD WITH FETA, OLIVES & QUINOA

This is one of Rob's favourite salads: it's super delicious, super healthy and fun to make (especially for those who like to get their hands a little messy!).   MAKES 4 SERVINGS

1 head radicchio, torn into pieces

½ acorn squash, roasted (see pages 25–26)

1 cup cooked quinoa

2 tablespoons crumbled feta

1 handful of green, black or mixed olives (pitted or not, up to you)

Extra virgin olive oil

Red wine vinegar

Fresh cracked black pepper

Arrange the radicchio evenly over a serving platter. Using your hands, pull the warm squash into pieces and place it overtop the radicchio. Sprinkle liberally with the quinoa, feta and olives. Drizzle with oil and a few dashes of red wine vinegar. Season with pepper to taste and serve (no salt needed—the feta and olives add enough salt).

POTATO SALAD WITH SQUASH, GRAINY MUSTARD & HERBS

This potato salad is low in fat and super flavourful thanks to the unique combination of grainy mustard and squash. The salad works best when the vinaigrette is tossed with the potatoes and squash as soon as they come out of the boiling water—the heat from the veggies helps them to soak up the vinaigrette.   MAKES 4 SERVINGS

½ small red onion, sliced

¼ teaspoon Dijon mustard

2 teaspoons grainy mustard

2 tablespoons extra virgin olive oil

2 teaspoons red wine vinegar

2 cups roasted cubed butternut squash (see page 25)

2 cups boiled cubed red potatoes (about 2 large potatoes)

Kosher salt and fresh cracked black pepper

Chopped fresh thyme, dill, tarragon or parsley, for garnish

In a bowl, combine the onion, Dijon mustard, grainy mustard, oil and vinegar to make the vinaigrette. Whisk together and set aside.

In a saucepan of boiling salted water, cook the squash until just tender. Using a slotted spoon, transfer the squash to a large serving bowl. Add the potatoes to the boiling water and cook just until tender. Transfer to the bowl with the squash.

Drizzle the squash and potatoes with the prepared vinaigrette and gently toss to coat. Season with salt and pepper to taste and sprinkle with the fresh herb of your choice. Serve warm or at room temperature.

PARMESAN-CRUSTED ACORN OVEN FRIES

Next time you have a hankering for potato wedges, try these! Rob's secret for this simple recipe is using a kitchen rasp to grate the Parmesan. The resulting tiny, fluffy gratings melt and form a crispy coating on the fries. The hot pepper flakes are optional but add a nice bit of heat that works well with the sweetness of the acorn squash.   MAKES 4 SERVINGS

1 medium acorn squash
Kosher salt and fresh cracked black
   pepper

1 teaspoon hot pepper flakes
½ cup finely grated Parmesan cheese

Preheat the oven to 400°F. Line a baking sheet with parchment paper.

Cut the acorn squash in half and remove the seeds (see page 20). Cut each half into 4 slices (for even slices, cut each half lengthwise down the middle, then take all 4 wedges and cut each one down the middle again). Sprinkle with salt and pepper to taste and finish with the hot pepper flakes.

Place the squash on the prepared baking sheet and bake in preheated oven for 20 minutes. Remove from the oven and sprinkle with the Parmesan. Reduce the oven temperature to 350°F and bake for 3 to 5 minutes, until cheese is melted. Serve hot from the oven.

OVERSTUFFED BAKED POTATO

Adding roasted squash to the stuffing for this baked potato means you can really pile it on! Try serving these with steaks or pork chops. We think the potato might just steal the spotlight. This recipe only calls for two potatoes but makes enough stuffing for four servings. Bake extra potatoes as needed.

MAKES 4 SERVINGS

1 acorn squash, halved and seeded
(see page 20)

2 large russet potatoes

2 tablespoons butter

1 green onion, white and green parts,
chopped

½ cup shredded cheddar cheese

¼ cup milk plus more if needed

Kosher salt and fresh cracked black
pepper

Preheat the oven to 375°F. Line a baking sheet with parchment paper.

Place the squash cut-side down on the prepared baking sheet and place in preheated oven. Place the potatoes directly on the middle oven rack beside the squash. Bake for 30 minutes, then check the squash: if soft, remove from the oven and scoop the hot flesh from one half into a bowl (use a kitchen towel or oven mitt to hold the hot squash while you do this). Reserve the other half for another use. Reserve the baking sheet with the parchment on it (you'll use it again later). Check the potatoes (they may need to bake for an additional 15 to 20 minutes, depending on size).

Once the potatoes are tender, remove from the oven and cut in half lengthwise. Scoop the flesh into the mixing bowl with the squash (use a kitchen towel or oven mitt to hold the hot potato while you do this). You should now have four potato "boats" ready to be stuffed. Place on the reserved baking sheet and set aside.

Add the butter, green onion and half of the cheese to the potato and squash mixture. Add the milk and mash until smooth, adding more milk if needed to achieve desired consistency. Season with salt and pepper to taste. Generously fill (overstuff) the potato "boats" with the mixture. Sprinkle with the remaining cheese. Bake for 5 minutes, until heated through and the cheese is melted. Serve immediately.

ACORN STUFFED FIVE WAYS

When Ivy was growing up, her dad, Rob Ethier, was fanatical about squash and would grow plenty of it in the garden and then store it in the root cellar over the winter. When her dad was making dinner, which he did often, a roasted acorn squash would always make an appearance. Stuffing a roasted acorn squash is easy, and there are endless variations. Here are five of our favourites. You can assemble the stuffing while the halved acorn squash is roasting. Once squash is done, remove from oven, add stuffing of your choice and return to oven for 6 to 8 minutes to warm through. MAKES 4 TO 6 SERVINGS

WHITE BEAN, BACON & SAGE

1 acorn squash, roasted (see pages 25–26)

2 strips bacon, cut into small matchsticks

1 cup canned white beans (cannellini, navy or white kidney beans), rinsed and drained

2 to 3 fresh sage leaves, finely chopped

Kosher salt and fresh cracked black pepper

Olive oil (optional)

In a frying pan over medium-high heat, cook the bacon until crispy, 5 to 8 minutes. Transfer bacon to a plate and add the beans to the pan. Lightly mash beans with a fork. Stir in the sage and season with salt and pepper to taste. Add a little oil if beans need moistening. Spoon into the roasted acorn squash.

QUINOA, ARUGULA & ROASTED PEPPER

1 acorn squash, roasted (see pages 25–26)

1 cup cooked quinoa

¼ cup chopped roasted red bell pepper (store-bought is fine)

1 handful of arugula

Kosher salt and fresh cracked black pepper

Olive oil (optional)

Combine the quinoa, roasted red pepper and arugula in a bowl and season with salt and pepper to taste. Add a little olive oil, if needed. Spoon into the roasted acorn squash.

COUSCOUS & LEMON WITH ROASTED GARLIC

1 acorn squash, roasted (see pages 25–26)

1 cup cooked couscous

Zest of 1 lemon

1 tablespoon roasted garlic
  (about 2 cloves)

2 teaspoons olive oil

Fresh lemon juice

Kosher salt and fresh cracked black
  pepper

Combine the couscous, lemon zest, garlic and oil in a bowl and season with lemon juice, salt and pepper to taste. Spoon into the roasted acorn squash.

APPLE, SAUSAGE & SWISS CHARD

1 acorn squash, roasted (see pages 25–26)

1 tablespoon olive oil

1 large pork sausage (French or Italian,
  not chorizo or brats)

1 bunch of Swiss chard, trimmed, ribs
  removed and chopped

1 Granny Smith apple, cored and chopped

Kosher salt and fresh cracked black
  pepper

In a frying pan, heat the oil over medium-high heat. Remove the sausage meat from its casing, add to the pan and cook through. Add the chard and sauté until just wilted, 2 to 3 minutes. Add the apple and stir to combine. Season with salt and pepper to taste. Spoon into the roasted acorn squash.

RYE BREAD, WALNUTS & CRANBERRIES

1 acorn squash, roasted (see pages 25–26)

1 tablespoon olive oil

½ small onion, finely diced

1 cup chopped toasted rye bread

¼ cup toasted walnuts, chopped
  (see Tip, page 88)

¼ cup dried cranberries, chopped

1 to 2 teaspoons water

Kosher salt and fresh cracked black
  pepper

In a frying pan, heat the oil over medium heat. Sauté the onion until softened, about 1½ minutes.
In a bowl, combine the bread, walnuts and cranberries. Add the water, just enough to wet the mixture for mashing. Season with salt and pepper to taste. Spoon into the roasted acorn squash.

BUTTERNUT CHUTNEY

This bright and colourful chutney gives a sweet and sour boost to fish or chicken and cooks up in only 10 minutes. We like to use it on Grilled Zucchini & Halibut Kebabs (page 102).

MAKES ABOUT 1½ CUPS

2 tablespoons olive oil

½ small onion, finely diced

1 cup finely diced butternut squash (see Tip)

1 cup chopped tomato

1 tablespoon white wine vinegar

2 tablespoons water

Kosher salt and fresh cracked black pepper

In a small saucepan, heat the oil over medium-high heat. Sauté the onion and squash until the onion starts to soften, about 1½ minutes. Stir in the tomato, vinegar and water and season with salt and pepper to taste. Reduce the heat to medium and cook, stirring occasionally, for 5 to 7 minutes, until the squash is tender. Remove from heat and set aside to cool. Will keep for up to 1 week in an airtight container in the refrigerator.

Tip: Compared with the bulb end (which contains the seeds), the neck of the butternut squash is easiest to cut into a small dice. It's also the easiest to peel. If you're in a real hurry, cut off the bulb and wrap and refrigerate for later use. Peel the neck and use what you need.

ROB'S PERFECT
GRILLED ZUCCHINI

This recipe is super simple and takes no time at all to put together but yields fantastic results, bringing out the best flavour that mild zucchini has to offer. Rob advises making it after your main dish is cooked and ready to go so the grilled zucchini is warm when served. Adding the olive oil after grilling (instead of before) is the secret to perfection when it comes to grilling zucchini. A clean, hot grill and dry zucchini ensure that it will not stick.

MAKES 2 SERVINGS

2 tablespoons olive oil

1 clove garlic, crushed

1 large or 2 small zucchini

Kosher salt and fresh cracked black
  pepper

Freshly grated Parmesan cheese (optional)

Chopped fresh chives (optional)

Get your grill nice and hot. Combine the oil and garlic in a small bowl and set aside.

Slice the zucchini lengthwise into three or four ¾-inch-thick batons. Pat the zucchini dry and grill until grill marks and blisters form, about 4 minutes each side. Remove from heat and brush with the garlic oil. Season with salt and pepper to taste. Sprinkle with Parmesan and chives (if using). Serve immediately.

SQUASH FRIED RICE

The secrets to great fried rice are medium heat and patience, so the rice has time to lose some of its moisture and get good and chewy. Be sure to keep scraping up and incorporating the delicious, caramelized crust that forms on the bottom of the pan while cooking, especially after stirring in the egg. Grating butternut squash right into the pan during the last 5 minutes of cooking ensures the squash keeps both its lovely colour and flavour and doesn't overcook. MAKES 4 SERVINGS

1 tablespoon sesame oil
1 tablespoon olive oil
2 cups cooked brown rice
2 tablespoons tamari
1 teaspoon freshly grated gingerroot
2 tablespoons green onion, white and green parts, chopped

½ yellow, orange or red bell pepper, seeded and chopped
4 shiitake mushrooms, sliced
1 egg, beaten
1½ cups freshly grated butternut squash
Fresh cracked black pepper

In a heavy-bottomed frying pan, heat the sesame and olive oils over medium heat. Sauté the rice for 10 minutes, stirring frequently. Stir in the tamari. Add the gingerroot, green onion, yellow pepper and mushrooms and mix well. Stir in the egg. Add the squash and cook, stirring frequently to scrape up any brown bits from the bottom of the pan, for 5 minutes. Season with additional tamari and black pepper to taste. Serve immediately.

CHEESY BAKED ACORN SQUASH & CAULIFLOWER CASSEROLE

This dish tastes like a rich soufflé but is much easier to make. You simply blitz up roasted veggies and top with cheese. We like to prepare it in a casserole dish, but you can also bake it in individual rame-kins for a fancier presentation. (Photo on pages 122–24.) **MAKES 6 TO 8 SERVINGS**

1 acorn squash, halved and seeded
   (see page 20)
Olive oil
1 head cauliflower, cut into florets
¼ cup milk

Kosher salt and fresh cracked black
   pepper
1 tablespoon butter
½ cup shredded cheddar cheese

Preheat the oven to 375°F. Line a baking sheet with parchment paper.

Sprinkle the squash with oil and place both halves cut-side down on the prepared baking sheet. Bake in preheated oven for 30 minutes.

Meanwhile, in a bowl, toss the cauliflower with salt and pepper to taste and a drizzle of oil. After the squash has been baking for 30 minutes, remove from the oven and add the seasoned cauliflower to the baking sheet with the squash. Return to the oven and bake for another 15 to 20 minutes, until the squash has softened and the cauliflower is lightly roasted and golden.

Scoop the hot acorn flesh from the skin and place in a food processor fitted with the metal blade or a blender. Add the roasted cauliflower and milk and purée until smooth (add more milk if needed to reach desired consistency). Season with salt and pepper to taste. (If needed, you can make the recipe up to this point and refrigerate overnight.)

Butter a casserole dish (or individual ramekins) and spoon in purée. Sprinkle evenly with the cheese. Bake for 15 to 20 minutes, until golden brown. Serve immediately. This dish is especially good served with the Kale Salad with Butternut Squash, Blue Cheese & Honey-Cider Vinaigrette on page 138.

CREAMY ACORN SQUASH POLENTA

The deep golden colour and sweet nutty flavour of roasted acorn squash adds a nice depth to classic polenta, keeping it rustic yet adding a touch of sophistication. This makes a perfect side to braised short ribs, a hearty ragout or osso buco.

MAKES 6 SERVINGS

1 tablespoon olive oil
½ onion, chopped
1 clove garlic, minced
1½ cups milk
1½ cups chicken stock
½ cup cornmeal

½ cup grated Parmesan cheese
1 cup mashed roasted acorn squash
  (see page 26)
Kosher salt and fresh cracked black
  pepper

In a medium saucepan, heat the oil over medium-high heat. Sauté the onion until softened, about 1½ minutes. Stir in the garlic. Add the milk and stock and bring to a simmer. In a slow, steady stream, whisk in the cornmeal, whisking constantly. The mixture will immediately begin to thicken; continue stirring with a wooden spoon. Reduce the heat and cook for 15 minutes, stirring often, until polenta reaches desired thickness. Remove from the heat. Add the cheese and squash and stir vigorously. Set aside to cool slightly. If the polenta thickens beyond desired consistency, stir in a little hot water, stock or milk or a tablespoon of butter. Season with salt and pepper to taste.

Tip: Spread any leftover polenta to a 1-inch thickness on parchment paper and cool completely. Then cut into slices, rounds or cubes and fry up the following day (delicious served with scrambled eggs at breakfast or as a side dish at dinner).

SPAGHETTI SQUASH WITH BLISTERED CHERRY TOMATOES & OLIVES

This is the kind of dish that shocks you with its simplicity and brilliance. It's delicious, super healthy, meat-free and almost fat-free. Spaghetti squash tends to leach liquid after roasting, so we suggest, for this recipe, that you drain it well before adding it to the pan. **MAKES 2 SERVINGS**

1 to 2 tablespoons olive oil, divided

15 to 20 cherry tomatoes

¼ cup mixed (green and black) olives

1½ cups roasted spaghetti squash, forked into "noodles" (see page 24)

Kosher salt and fresh cracked black pepper

In a heavy-bottomed frying pan (cast-iron is best), heat 1 tablespoon oil over medium-high heat. Add the cherry tomatoes and cook, stirring constantly, until their skins start to blister. Add the olives and spaghetti squash and a drizzle of oil. Toss well and sauté until the squash is heated through, 3 to 5 minutes. Season with salt and pepper to taste. Serve warm.

ZUCCHINI & OPO SQUASH SUCCOTASH

Although opo squash (also known as long squash) is popular in South Asian and Chinese cooking, in North America it deserves more attention. The longer it is left on the vine to grow, the more bitter it gets, but when it is young it has a bright, crisp flavour that is wonderful in succotash. It is a perfect accompaniment to pan-fried fish or pork chops, and a nice break from potatoes. The zucchini and opo squash in this version give it pizzazz, colour and crunch. **MAKES 4 SERVINGS**

1 small zucchini, cut into 2-inch-long batons (about ½ inch thick)

1 small long (opo) squash, cut into 2-inch-long batons (about ½ inch thick)

3 teaspoons olive oil, divided

Kosher salt and fresh cracked black pepper

¼ cup diced red bell pepper

½ cup frozen lima beans

½ cup frozen corn kernels

1 green onion, white and green parts, chopped

In a bowl, toss together the zucchini, long squash, 2 teaspoons oil and a sprinkling of salt and pepper. **Heat** a frying pan over medium-high heat and cook the squash mixture in batches (so as not to crowd the pan) until lightly browned. As the batches are cooked, transfer to a plate and set aside.

In the same frying pan, heat the remaining 1 teaspoon oil. Sauté the red pepper, lima beans, corn and green onion for 5 to 7 minutes, until the red pepper softens. Return the squash mixture to the pan, stir well, then cover and cook for 2 minutes, until warmed through.

BRUSSELS SPROUTS, SQUASH & BACON

Bacon and squash are a match made in heaven, and when combined with Brussels sprouts, they make a hearty side dish. We cut the bacon into fat little matchsticks and cook them up nice and crispy so they add their bacon love to every bite.   **MAKES 4 SERVINGS**

2 strips bacon, cut into thick matchsticks
10 Brussels sprouts, halved
1 cup roasted cubed butternut squash
    (see page 25)

Kosher salt and fresh cracked black
    pepper
Knob of butter

Preheat the oven to 375°F.

In an oven-proof frying pan over medium-high heat, sauté the bacon until crispy, about 5 minutes. Transfer the bacon to a plate, reserving bacon fat in pan.

To the same pan, add the Brussels sprouts and squash, toss to coat well with reserved bacon fat and season with salt and pepper to taste. Add the butter and bake in preheated oven for 7 minutes. Remove from the oven and stir in the reserved bacon. Bake for an additional 3 to 5 minutes, until squash and Brussels sprouts are tender.

TEN-MINUTE RISOTTO

Risotto doesn't make regular appearances on the average dinner table because it requires a lot of stirring and attention. Our friend Fenwick Bonnell, an accomplished home cook, loves risotto but hates the stirring (doesn't that sound like the lead-in to an infomercial?), so he decided to cheat and cook the Arborio rice just like pasta. Guess what? It works: a lovely risotto flavoured with the fresh, clean taste of zucchini on the table in just 10 minutes. MAKES 4 SERVINGS

1 cup Arborio rice
1 tablespoon olive oil
1 zucchini, cubed

1 tablespoon butter
Freshly grated Parmesan cheese
Kosher salt and fresh cracked black
pepper

In a pot of boiling salted water, cook the rice for 10 minutes (check for doneness the same way you would pasta).

Meanwhile, heat a sauté pan over medium-high heat. Add the oil and zucchini and sauté until browned, about 5 minutes.

As soon as the rice is ready, strain and add it to the pan with the zucchini. Stir well to combine. Add the butter and Parmesan to taste. Stir well and season with salt and pepper to taste. Serve immediately.

ZUCCHINI À LA CAPONATA

This Sicilian salad has a motley list of ingredients that only seem odd together until you taste them. Sweet and sour components combine in a way that is uniquely Italian.   MAKES 4 SERVINGS

1 small eggplant, cubed (½ inch)

2 teaspoons olive oil, divided

Kosher salt and fresh cracked black pepper

1 zucchini, cubed (½ inch)

15 to 20 cherry tomatoes

¼ cup diced red bell pepper

¼ cup green olives, pitted and roughly chopped

1 tablespoon currants

Zest of 1 lemon

1 tablespoon red wine vinegar

1 tablespoon extra virgin olive oil

Fresh lemon juice (optional)

1 bunch of fresh basil leaves, roughly chopped or torn

Heat the oven to 425°F. Line a baking sheet with parchment paper.

In a bowl, toss the eggplant with 1 teaspoon oil and season with salt and pepper to taste. Spread the eggplant over the prepared baking sheet and bake in preheated oven for 8 to 10 minutes, until browned and softened.

Meanwhile, toss the zucchini with the remaining 1 teaspoon oil and season with salt and pepper to taste.

Heat a frying pan over medium-high heat and sauté seasoned zucchini, until just browned. (The zucchini only needs to brown on one side. It may not appear to be fully cooked, but it will finish cooking as it cools.)

Transfer the cooked zucchini to a bowl. Add the baked eggplant, tomatoes, red pepper, olives, currants and lemon zest. Drizzle with the red wine vinegar and oil and toss to combine. Let sit at room temperature for 1 hour to allow flavours to meld. Taste and, if needed, season with additional salt and pepper or lemon juice or red wine vinegar. Just before serving, stir in the basil. Serve at room temperature.

Tip: We use regular olive oil to cook the eggplant and zucchini, then extra virgin for finishing the dish.

SPAGHETTI SQUASH
PUTTANESCA

Puttanesca sauce usually calls for anchovy filets, but we like to make it vegan, tossing it with hearty spaghetti squash "noodles." Using these "noodles" makes the dish gluten-free and adds a lovely flavour that you wouldn't get from regular spaghetti noodles. **MAKES 4 SERVINGS**

1 tablespoon olive oil

1 onion, chopped

1 clove garlic

1 can (28 oz) tomato sauce (store-bought is fine)

¼ cup pitted chopped mixed olives (black and green)

2 tablespoons capers, drained and chopped

2 tablespoons basil pesto (store-bought is fine)

½ teaspoon hot pepper flakes

Kosher salt and fresh cracked black pepper

1 roasted spaghetti squash, forked into "noodles" (see page 24)

In a large saucepan, heat the oil over medium heat. Sauté the onion until softened, about 1½ minutes. Add the garlic and cook until fragrant, about 1 minute. Add the tomato sauce, olives, capers, pesto, and hot pepper flakes and season with salt and pepper to taste. Simmer for 20 minutes or until thickened.

If the spaghetti squash is hot straight from the oven, you can toss the strands in a little oil, season with salt and pepper to taste, divide among serving plates and top with the sauce. If the squash was cooked in advance and needs warming, simply sauté the strands in a frying pan with a bit of oil, season with salt and pepper, then plate and top with sauce.

ZIPPY ZUCCHINI
REFRIGERATOR PICKLES

Had another bumper crop of zucchini? You can make these refrigerator pickles in less than 10 minutes, and they'll keep for up to 3 weeks in the fridge. (Photo on pages 122–24.)   MAKES 1 QUART

1 Mason jar (32 oz), sterilized in boiling water

3 cups zucchini (about 2 medium zucchini) cut into ⅛-inch-thick coins or sliced into ribbons

1 cup apple cider vinegar

3 tablespoons granulated sugar

1 tablespoon kosher salt

2 teaspoons yellow mustard seeds

1 teaspoon hot pepper flakes

1 teaspoon ground turmeric

1 cup boiling water

Put a kettle of water on to boil.

Meanwhile, pack the zucchini into the Mason jar.

In a bowl, whisk together the vinegar, sugar, salt, mustard seeds, hot pepper flakes and turmeric. Pour in the boiling water and whisk well. Pour the vinegar mixture over the zucchini (leaving at least 1 inch headspace), seal tightly and let cool completely before refrigerating. Refrigerate 24 hours before serving.

Manganese, Please

Summer squash, such as a medium-sized
zucchini or pattypan, contain about one-quarter
of our daily manganese requirement. Manganese
is essential for bone health, healthy skin and
brain function. Sauté sliced zucchini for a
savoury side dish or slip some into
soup to get your fix.

BREADS & DESSERTS

Squash and pumpkin are wonderful flavour bases for breads and desserts. Their rich and nutty taste marries perfectly with warm spices like nutmeg, clove and cinnamon. Their natural sweetness is intensified, and hints of caramel, nuts and rum become more pronounced.

When you include squash in any dish you benefit from the amazingly high concentration of vitamins and minerals they contain. So try them in these breads and sweet treats, and feel a little less guilty about the indulgence.

Clockwise from top left: Cheesy Squashy Cornbread (page 194); Zucchini, Orange & Pumpkin Seed Muffins (page 189); Pumpkin Cupcakes (page 180); Lemon & Pumpkin Custards (page 178); and Butternut Squares (page 188).

SQUASHSICLES

These Middle Eastern–inspired popsicles are creamy and sweet, and super fast to whip up. No ice-cream maker required, just a whisk and a popsicle mould.   **MAKES 8 POPSICLES**

1 cup sweetened condensed milk

¾ cup evaporated milk

½ cup whipping (35%) cream

½ cup canned unsweetened pumpkin
  purée

½ teaspoon ground ginger

½ teaspoon ground cinnamon

¼ teaspoon ground nutmeg

In a mixing bowl, whisk together all of the ingredients. Pour into popsicle moulds. Be careful to leave about ¼ inch headspace to allow the mixture to expand as it freezes. Insert popsicle stick or lids and freeze for 6 to 8 hours or overnight.

CANDIED BUTTERNUT SUNDAE

This is a slightly grown-up take on a hot fudge sundae, with hot candied squash stepping in for the fudge sauce. This recipe makes about a quart of candied butternut, which is also spectacular on toast, pancakes and waffles (a small Mason jar filled with it makes a lovely little gift).

MAKES ABOUT 1 QUART

¼ cup plus 2 tablespoons orange
  marmalade
⅓ cup granulated sugar
Pinch of ground nutmeg
2 tablespoons fresh lemon juice
2½ cups water

1 small butternut squash, peeled, seeded
  and cut into ½-inch cubes
  (about 4 cups)
French vanilla ice cream
Roasted pepitas (see page 26)

In a large pot over medium-high heat, combine the marmalade, sugar, nutmeg and lemon juice. Stir in the water. Bring to a boil, stirring constantly until sugar is dissolved. Add the squash and stir to combine. Return the mixture to a boil. Reduce the heat to medium-low and simmer, partially covered, stirring occasionally, until the squash is tender when pierced with a fork, about 35 minutes. Uncover and cook until the liquid is syrupy, 5 to 10 minutes. Remove from heat and set aside to cool slightly.

Scoop good-quality French vanilla ice cream into your favourite parfait glass, top with a large spoonful of warm candied butternut and finish with crunchy roasted pepitas. Serve immediately.

The candied squash can be refrigerated in an airtight container for up to 1 week. Reheat over medium-low heat before serving. If the syrup seems too thick, stir in 1 to 2 tablespoons water.

LEMON & PUMPKIN CUSTARDS

The tang of fresh lemon juice married with rich, smooth pumpkin makes this dessert a real show-stopper. You may want to double the recipe when making this—these custards do not last long. (Photo on pages 170–72.)

MAKES 6 SERVINGS

½ cup fresh lemon juice

1 tablespoon lemon zest

1 tablespoon orange zest

⅔ cup granulated sugar

¼ cup lightly packed brown sugar

1 whole egg

4 egg yolks

½ cup canned unsweetened pumpkin purée

1½ cups whipping (35%) cream

Fresh raspberries or blueberries

Preheat the oven to 325°F. Arrange 6 oven-proof custard bowls in a deep baking dish.

Bring a kettle of water to a boil. Carefully pour boiling water into the baking dish, halfway up the sides of the custard bowls (to make a bain-marie), making sure not to splash any water into the custard bowls.

In a mixing bowl, combine the lemon juice and zest, orange zest, sugars, egg and egg yolks, pumpkin and cream and mix on high speed, about 1 minute.

Pour the mixture into the custard bowls, filling almost to the brim but not quite. Bake in preheated oven for 45 minutes. Remove from the oven and set aside to cool completely and set (they will be wobbly but not sloppy). Refrigerate to chill completely before serving. Serve chilled topped with fresh berries.

Tip: A bain-marie (hot water bath) is a great way to keep thick liquids that set when cooled— sauces, custard, melted chocolate, etc.—in their liquid states, and it also helps foods like custards to cook more evenly in the oven. In this dish, the bain-marie keeps the sides and bottoms of the custards from cooking too quickly.

PUMPKIN PANNA COTTA

Bertrand Alépée, a French-trained chef and pastry chef, is the owner of The Tempered Chef, a catering and consulting company in Toronto. He created this dessert for Canoe restaurant and was kind enough to share it with us. If you can't find the Szechwan pepper included in the caramel, you can leave it out. The dessert will still be divine; it just won't have that spicy kick.

MAKES 12 PANNA COTTA

Panna Cotta
10 gelatin sheets
4 cups milk
2 cups whipping (35%) cream
1 teaspoon pure vanilla extract
1 cup granulated sugar
1⅓ cups canned unsweetened pumpkin
  purée

Szechwan Caramel
1⅓ cups granulated sugar
⅓ cup glucose or white corn syrup
Water
1 tablespoon Szechwan pepper
1 cup whipping (35%) cream

Prepare the panna cotta: In a small bowl, submerge the gelatin in ice-cold water and set aside for 1 minute to "bloom."

In a saucepan over medium heat, combine the milk, cream, vanilla and sugar and bring to a boil. Remove the pan from the heat and whisk in the bloomed gelatin. Whisk in the pumpkin purée, then strain the mixture through a fine-mesh sieve into a bowl to remove any solids. Pour into 12 ramekins or foil cups (with ½ cup capacity) until three-quarters full and refrigerate for at least 4 hours to chill.

Prepare the Szechwan caramel: In another saucepan over medium heat, combine the sugar, glucose and just enough water to dissolve everything. Cook without stirring, brushing the sides of the pan with a pastry brush dipped in warm water to prevent the sugar from crystallizing, until the mixture turns a nice caramel colour. Stir in the Szechwan pepper. Add the cream and bring to a boil, stirring often, until the caramel is nice and uniform in consistency. Remove the pan from the heat and set aside for 30 minutes to allow all the flavours to meld, then strain through a fine-mesh sieve. Set aside to cool to room temperature.

To unmould the panna cotta, run a knife around the inside edge of each ramekin, dip the bottom of the ramekin into warm water and then invert the ramekin onto individual serving plates. To serve, drizzle the panna cotta with Szechwan caramel sauce.

PUMPKIN CUPCAKES

Containing just a little ginger and spice, and frosted with Rum-pum Pumpkin Cream Cheese Icing (recipe follows), these are just the right cupcakes for any occasion. MAKES 12 CUPCAKES

⅓ cup butter, softened

1 cup granulated sugar

2 eggs

1¼ cups canned unsweetened pumpkin
   purée

2 cups all-purpose flour

¼ teaspoon kosher salt

1½ teaspoons baking powder

1 teaspoon baking soda

1 teaspoon ground allspice

1 teaspoon ground cinnamon

1 teaspoon ground ginger

Preheat the oven to 350°F. Line a 12-cup muffin pan with paper liners.

In a mixing bowl, cream together the butter and sugar until light and fluffy. Add the eggs and pumpkin and mix well.

In another bowl, sift together the flour, salt, baking powder, baking soda, allspice, cinnamon and ginger. Add to the wet ingredients in three batches, mixing well to incorporate each batch before adding more. Mix until the batter is light and creamy, about 2 minutes.

Spoon the batter into the muffin cups until three-quarters full. Bake in preheated oven for 25 minutes or until a toothpick poked into the centre of a cupcake comes out clean. Remove from the oven and let cool in pan for 5 minutes, then transfer to a wire rack to cool completely.

Frost with Rum-pum Pumpkin Cream Cheese Icing (recipe follows).

RUM-PUM PUMPKIN CREAM CHEESE ICING
MAKES ENOUGH TO GENEROUSLY FROST 12 LARGE CUPCAKES

⅓ cup cream cheese, softened

⅓ cup butter, softened

⅓ cup canned unsweetened pumpkin
   purée

2 tablespoons dark rum

1¾ cups icing (confectioner's) sugar

In a mixing bowl, cream together the cream cheese and butter. Mix in the pumpkin and rum until well combined. In three batches, add the icing sugar, mixing well to incorporate each batch before adding more. Beat until creamy, 2 to 3 minutes.

MINI PUMPKIN TARTS WITH BRANDIED WHIPPED CREAM

Ivy was first introduced to brandied cream while cooking at Chez Piggy, in Kingston, Ontario, where they serve it with strawberry shortcake. You can make your own pastry for these tarts or use frozen tart shells and just follow the instructions on the package.   MAKES 24 TARTS

24 frozen tart shells
2 eggs
1 can (28 oz) unsweetened pumpkin
   purée
1 cup lightly packed brown sugar

1 teaspoon ground cinnamon
1 teaspoon ground nutmeg
1 teaspoon ground ginger
¼ teaspoon kosher salt
¾ cup evaporated milk

Preheat the oven to 425°F. Arrange the frozen tart shells on a baking sheet.
In a mixing bowl, beat the eggs. Add the pumpkin, sugar, cinnamon, nutmeg, ginger and salt and mix well. Add the milk and mix well. Spoon the mixture into the tart shells, filling completely. Bake in preheated oven for 15 minutes, then reduce the heat to 350°F and continue baking for another 20 minutes or until a toothpick poked into the centre of a tart comes out clean. Remove from the oven and set aside to cool completely. Serve with brandied whipped cream (recipe follows).

BRANDIED WHIPPPED CREAM
MAKES ABOUT 4 CUPS

1 cup whipping (35%) cream
2 teaspoons granulated sugar

½ teaspoon pure vanilla extract
½ ounce brandy

In a mixing bowl, whip cream, sugar and vanilla until soft peaks form. Fold in brandy. Keep refrigerated until ready to serve.

BUTTERNUT BROWNIES

It might sound strange, but adding butternut squash is the key to absolutely scrumptious brownies. The delicate squash flavour is overshadowed by the chocolate, but you won't believe the difference its presence makes to these moist and rich brownies.   **MAKES 16 BROWNIES**

1½ cups diced (¼ to ½ inch) butternut squash

6 tablespoons butter

6 ounces semisweet chocolate, chopped

¼ cup unsweetened cocoa powder

¾ cups all-purpose flour

½ teaspoon kosher salt

¼ teaspoon baking powder

1 cup granulated sugar

2 eggs

2 teaspoons pure vanilla extract

Preheat the oven to 350°F. Grease an 8-inch square baking pan or line it with parchment paper, allowing a few inches to hang over each side. Butter the parchment paper (if using) and set pan aside.

Bring a saucepan filled with enough water to cover squash to a rolling boil, then add squash and cook for 6 to 10 minutes, or until tender. Drain well and set aside.

In a double boiler over medium-high heat, combine the butter, chocolate and cocoa powder, stirring constantly until smooth. Remove from heat and set aside.

In a separate bowl, whisk together the flour, salt and baking powder.

In a mixing bowl, cream together the sugar, eggs and vanilla. Add the chocolate mixture and mix until combined. Add the flour mixture and mix until well blended. Fold in the squash.

Pour the batter into the prepared pan. Bake in preheated oven for 35 to 40 minutes or until a toothpick poked in the centre comes out clean (a little melted chocolate is fine!). Remove from the oven and cool in the pan for about 15 minutes.

Grab the ends of the parchment paper and lift the slab from the pan. Place on a wire rack to cool completely before cutting into squares.

BUTTERNUT CRANBERRY PUDDING CAKE

Maple syrup makes this rich pudding cake a quintessentially Canadian experience, and the ruby red cranberries and little golden butternut nuggets make it as beautiful to look at as it is to taste.

MAKES 1 CAKE

1 cup fresh or frozen cranberries

1 cup diced (½ inch) butternut squash

1 cup pure maple syrup

⅔ cup whipping (35%) cream

¾ teaspoon orange zest

½ teaspoon kosher salt

⅔ cup all-purpose flour

⅓ cup cornmeal

1½ teaspoons baking powder

½ teaspoon kosher salt

1 egg

3 tablespoons granulated sugar

½ cup milk

½ cup butter, melted

1 teaspoon pure vanilla extract

Crème fraîche or whipped cream

Preheat the oven to 400°F.

In a saucepan over medium-high heat, combine the cranberries, squash, maple syrup, cream, orange zest and a pinch of salt. Bring to a boil, stirring occasionally, then reduce the heat and simmer for 1 minute. Remove from heat and set aside.

In a bowl, whisk together the flour, cornmeal, baking powder and salt.

In a large bowl, whisk together the egg and sugar. Add the milk, butter and vanilla and mix well. Add the flour mixture and whisk to blend.

Pour the warm cranberry mixture into a 9- x 9-inch pan. Pour the batter overtop. Bake in preheated oven until golden and cranberry mixture bubbles around the edges, about 20 to 25 minutes. Remove from the oven and set aside to cool for 15 minutes.

Serve topped with crème fraîche or whipped cream.

BUTTERNUT SQUARES

These squares are inspired by Ivy's grandmother, Marthe Mailloux, née Bois, who is famous for her date squares. These are similar to date squares, but with the tops removed and the dates replaced by squash that's been infused with grapefruit and orange juice. The tangy, bright yellow-orange squash filling is a delicious change from the traditional dates. (Photo on pages 170–72.)

MAKES 24 SQUARES

Filling

2 cups mashed roasted butternut squash
   (see page 26)

½ cup water

½ cup grapefruit juice

⅓ cup granulated sugar

2 teaspoons fresh lemon juice

1 teaspoon pure vanilla extract

Rind of 1 orange

Pinch of salt

Crust

½ cup butter, softened

¾ cup all-purpose flour

¾ cup quick-cooking rolled oats

¾ cup lightly packed brown sugar

¼ teaspoon baking soda

Make the filling: In a saucepan over medium-high heat, combine all of the ingredients for the filling and cook until the squash is tender, about 25 minutes. Remove from the heat and mash until the mixture reaches a smooth, purée-like consistency. If the mixture is too runny, cook over low heat, stirring occasionally, until the desired consistency is reached. Set aside.

Make the crust: Preheat the oven to 350°F. Butter a 9- × 13-inch baking pan. In a mixing bowl, add all of the ingredients for the crust and mix with a spoon or your hands until well combined.

Press half of the crust mixture evenly over the bottom of the prepared baking pan. Spread the filling evenly over the crust. Sprinkle the remaining crust mixture overtop and pat down lightly. Bake in preheated oven for 40 minutes. Remove from the oven and cool completely before cutting into squares and removing from the pan (cut them as big or as small as you like!). Will keep in an airtight container at room temperature for up to 4 days.

ZUCCHINI, ORANGE & PUMPKIN SEED MUFFINS

Zucchini adds a pop of colour and candied orange peel lends a festive flavour to these healthy muffins. (Photo on pages 170–72.)

MAKES 12 MUFFINS

½ cup butter, softened
⅓ cup lightly packed brown sugar
½ cup buttermilk
2 eggs
1 teaspoon pure vanilla extract
1 medium zucchini, grated
¼ cup candied orange peel

¼ cup roasted pumpkin seeds, chopped (see Tip)
½ cup old-fashioned rolled oats
¾ cup all-purpose flour
¾ cup whole-wheat flour
1 teaspoon baking powder
1 teaspoon baking soda
½ teaspoon kosher salt

Preheat the oven to 375°F. Line a 12-cup muffin pan with paper liners.

In a mixing bowl, cream together the butter and sugar. Mix in the buttermilk and eggs. Add the vanilla, zucchini, orange peel and pumpkin seeds and mix well.

In another bowl, combine the oats, flours, baking powder, baking soda and salt. Add to the wet ingredients and stir just to combine (do not over-stir or the muffins will be tough and dense).

Fill each muffin cup three-quarters full. Bake in preheated oven for 15 to 20 minutes or until a toothpick poked in the centre of a muffin comes out clean. Turn out onto a wire rack to cool completely. Will keep in an airtight container for up to 4 days; also freezes well.

Tip: If you substitute pepitas for full-size pumpkin seeds, you won't need to chop them.

ZUCCHINI WALNUT LOAF
WITH LEMON GLAZE

An updated version of a classic tea bread, Kerry's zucchini loaf is sophisticated and elegant enough to serve at one of his mom's bridge parties. The addition of zucchini ensures that the end result is tender and moist.

MAKES 1 LOAF

Loaf
½ cup unsalted butter, softened
½ cup lightly packed brown sugar
½ cup granulated sugar
2 eggs
1¼ cups plain yogurt
1 tablespoon lemon zest
2 teaspoons almond oil
1 teaspoon pure vanilla extract
1 medium or 2 small zucchini, grated
1½ cups all-purpose flour
1 cup whole-wheat flour

1 teaspoon baking powder
1 teaspoon ground cinnamon
1 teaspoon ground ginger
½ teaspoon baking soda
½ teaspoon kosher salt
½ cup currants
½ cup walnut pieces

Glaze
2 cups icing (confectioner's) sugar
Zest of 1 lemon and 1 orange
4 tablespoons fresh lemon juice

Preheat the oven to 350°F. Butter a 9- × 5-inch loaf pan and lightly dust with flour.

In a mixing bowl, cream together the butter, sugars and eggs. Mix in the yogurt, lemon zest, almond oil and vanilla. Mix in the zucchini.

In another bowl, sift together the flours, baking powder, cinnamon, ginger, baking soda and salt. Add to wet ingredients in three batches, mixing well to incorporate each batch before adding more. Fold in the currants and nuts. Scrape the batter into the prepared loaf pan and bake in preheated oven for 60 minutes or until a toothpick poked in the centre comes out clean.

Remove from the oven and let loaf cool in pan for 15 minutes before tipping onto a plate.

Meanwhile, make the glaze: In a bowl, combine the icing sugar, half of the lemon and orange zest, and lemon juice and mix until smooth.

When the loaf has completely cooled, drizzle the glaze overtop and sprinkle with the remaining lemon and orange zest. Will keep in an airtight container at room temperature for up to 4 days.

HUBBARD MOLASSES BREAD

This tasty bread was inspired by a recipe of Kerry's mother, Joan. Kerry made this recipe his own by adding sunflower seeds and roasted hubbard squash. The bread is very hearty, and each slice demands a great slathering of butter for maximum enjoyment.

MAKES 3 LOAVES (OR 2 LOAVES AND 12 BUNS)

2 packages active dry yeast (1 package = about 2¼ teaspoons = ¼ ounce)

1 teaspoon granulated sugar

½ cup warm water

1½ cups cooked oatmeal, cooled

2 teaspoons kosher salt

1 tablespoon butter, softened

¼ cup blackstrap molasses

1½ cups puréed roasted hubbard squash (see page 26)

6 cups whole-wheat flour

½ cup roasted unsalted shelled sunflower seeds

In a small bowl, combine yeast, sugar and water and set aside until "proofed" and bubbling, about 5 minutes.

In a mixing bowl, combine proofed yeast, prepared oatmeal, salt, butter, molasses and squash. Add flour, 1 cup at a time, mixing well to incorporate into each batch before adding more. Fold in the sunflower seeds. Turn the dough out onto a floured work surface and knead until the dough is tacky but not sticky, about 10 minutes. (Alternatively, you can use the paddle attachment on a stand mixer and mix for 10 minutes.) Place the dough in a lightly oiled bowl, cover with a kitchen towel and set aside in a warm place until doubled in bulk, about 2 hours.

Punch down dough and divide into 3 equal portions. Shape into loaves (or buns; see page 193). Place loaves in buttered loaf pans, cover and set aside until doubled in bulk, about 45 minutes.

Preheat the oven to 400°F.

Bake on middle rack of preheated oven for 15 minutes. Reduce the heat to 375°F and continue baking for 15 to 20 minutes or until a toothpick poked in the centre comes out clean.

Remove from the oven and turn out onto a wire rack to cool. Will keep in an airtight container for up to 4 days.

HUBBARD MOLASSES BUNS

Ivy likes to keep the dough for one loaf of Hubbard Molasses Bread to make into buns. Great for lunch snacks or to eat on the run. MAKES 12 BUNS

Dough for 1 loaf Hubbard Molasses Bread
(see page 192)

Make the dough as outlined in preceding recipe. Before the second rise, shape the dough into 12 balls. (To make clover-leaf shapes, make 36 small balls—3 small balls per muffin cup.)

Place the balls in the buttered cups of a 12-cup muffin pan. Set aside in a warm place until doubled in bulk, about 45 minutes.

Bake in a preheated 375°F oven for 15 minutes, reduce the heat to 350°F and continue baking for about 10 minutes, until a toothpick poked in the centre of a bun comes out clean.

Remove from the oven and turn buns out onto a wire rack to cool.

CINNAMON RAISIN BREAD

When making Hubbard Molasses Bread, we like to earmark one-third of the dough for cinnamon raisin bread. Served hot with a generous amount of butter, it may be the best breakfast toast ever.
MAKES 1 LOAF

Dough for 1 loaf Hubbard Molasses Bread
(see page 192)
½ cup raisins

¼ cup lightly packed brown sugar
1 teaspoon ground cinnamon

Make the dough as outlined in the Hubbard Molasses Bread recipe (page 192). After the dough's first rise, knead in ½ cup raisins. Using a rolling pin, roll out the dough in a rough square, about 1 inch thick.

In a bowl, combine the sugar and cinnamon. Sprinkle mixture overtop the dough. Roll up the dough and place in buttered loaf pan.

Bake on middle rack of preheated 400°F oven for 15 minutes. Reduce the heat to 375°F and continue baking for 15 to 20 minutes, until a toothpick poked in the centre of the loaf comes out clean.

Remove from the oven and turn out onto a wire rack to cool.

CHEESY SQUASHY CORNBREAD

There is a little magic in this recipe, and it comes from a touch of honey in the bread, which balances beautifully with the green onions. The squash and olive oil keep this toothsome cornbread moist with the perfect crumb. (Photo on pages 170–72.)

MAKES 1 LOAF

1 egg

2 tablespoons liquid honey

1 cup milk

¼ cup olive oil

2 green onions, white and green parts, chopped

1 cup all-purpose flour

1 cup cornmeal

3 teaspoons baking powder

½ teaspoon kosher salt

1 cup roasted cubed acorn or butternut squash (see page 25)

½ cup shredded sharp (old) cheddar cheese

Preheat the oven to 375°F. Butter an 8- × 8-inch square baking pan or 9-inch cast-iron frying pan.

In a mixing bowl, combine the egg, honey, milk, oil and green onions.

In another bowl, combine the flour, cornmeal, baking powder and salt. Add to the wet ingredients and mix until just combined. Fold in the squash and cheese. Spread the batter into the prepared baking pan. Bake in preheated oven for 25 to 30 minutes or until a toothpick poked in the centre comes out clean. Set aside to cool in pan before turning out. Will keep in an airtight container at room temperature for up to 4 days.

ACKNOWLEDGEMENTS

The authors would like to thank our editor Brad Wilson, copy editor Tracy Bordian, managing editor Noelle Zitzer, page designer Greg Tabor and cover designer Lisa Bettencourt. Special thanks to David Kent, Iris Tupholme, Leo MacDonald, Sandra Leef, Michael Guy-Haddock and Peter Borcsok for all their support. We would also like to thank Reena Newman for the recipe photos, Chantal Payette for her food styling, Phillipa Croft of Phillipa C. Photography for her great author shots, and Christopher Campbell and Pat Crocker for additional squash photography. We're grateful to the interns who worked on the shoot for the book: Katrina Johns, Jennifer Benson and Karen Eisenberg.

Thanks to all of our families—Knights, Firings, Zitzers, Ethiers, Curries and Maillouxs—especially to Ivy's squash-obsessed father, Rob Ethier. His passion for serving squash with every single meal ensured that she was suited to take on this project. We're eternally grateful to Kerry's mom, Joan, for passing her baking skills down to him. It is of much more value to us than the family silver. Thanks to Rob's mum, Sherry, for her passion for cooking and gardening, and to Jack Kirchhoff for his recipe suggestions.

Much thanks to the industry folk for sharing recipes and techniques: Bertrand Alépée, Anthony Rose, Rossy Earle and Alexandra Feswick. Thank you, Lauren Wilton, for the loan of your Le Creuset collection for our recipe testing and photo shoots.

Thanks to our friends who taste-tested along with us as we cooked our way through all the recipes: Beverly Crandon, Ana Gervasio, Fenwick Bonnell, Phillipa Croft, Arlene Stein, Jenny Duquette, Jimmy Felix and Kaet Duquette. And to Poppy, Betty and Peabody, who ate all the flops—good thing our dogs love squash!

An especially big thank-you to Michael Smith, Laura Calder and Lynn Crawford, who all gave advice and encouragement when it was needed.

INDEX